Multiple Choice Practice Tests in Mathematics for CSEC®

Fayad W. Ali

Nelson Thornes
Part of Oxford University Press

OXFORD
UNIVERSITY PRESS

Great Clarendon Street, Oxford, OX2 6DP, United Kingdom

Oxford University Press is a department of the University of Oxford.
It furthers the University's objective of excellence in research, scholarship,
and education by publishing worldwide. Oxford is a registered trade mark of
Oxford University Press in the UK and in certain other countries

First published by Thomas Nelson and Sons Ltd in 2000
This edition first published by Nelson Thornes Ltd in 2004

British Library Cataloguing in Publication Data
Data available

978-0-17-566457-3

20

Printed in Great Britain by CPI Group (UK) Ltd., Croydon CR0 4YY

Acknowledgements

Page make-up: Upstream, London

Text and cover design by Barker/Hilsden

This book is dedicated to Naparima College

Although we have made every effort to trace and contact all copyright
holders before publication this has not been possible in all cases.
If notified, the publisher will rectify any errors or omissions at the
earliest opportunity.

Links to third party websites are provided by Oxford in good faith
and for information only. Oxford disclaims any responsibility for
the materials contained in any third party website referenced in
this work.

Preface

This book of 12 Multiple Choice Practice Tests was designed especially for students preparing for the CSEC General Proficiency Examinations in Mathematics at the Ordinary Level.

The questions on the various topics may vary in difficulty from test to test, but in general the tests are all challenging and require in-depth thinking and reasoning.

Students may wish to follow various approaches in doing the tests. They may be used:

- as a classroom exercise

- as an exercise involving a study group

- as an individual exercise

At the end of each test, students are advised to revise the topics which may have presented any degree of difficulty. This will enable them to be better prepared to solve similar problems, including more difficult ones that might appear in other test or in the examination itself.

Whatever method or combination of methods students decide to adopt, it is recommended that these tests be done on the completion of a full mathematics course. Answers should be verified upon completion of the entire test. A systematic approach is strongly recommended, that is, when tests are complete, checks be made for improvements in time, accuracy and general performance.

The author wishes to express his sincere gratitude to all persons who supported, advised and assisted in any way towards this publication.

Fayad W. Ali
Head of Mathematics
Naparima College
Trinidad
West Indies

Directions for candidates

Test number 1

Read the directions on page (iv) carefully.

1 0.005 28 in standard form is

- **A** 5.28×10^{-5} Ⓐ
- **B** 5.28×10^{-3} Ⓑ
- **C** 5.28×10^{-2} Ⓒ
- **D** 5.28×10^{3} Ⓓ

2 The first four multiples of 5 are

- **A** 4, 9, 14, 19 Ⓐ
- **B** 5, 10, 15, 20 Ⓑ
- **C** 1, 5, 25, 125 Ⓒ
- **D** 5, 50, 500, 5000 Ⓓ

3 If 40% of a number is 80, the number is

- **A** 2 Ⓐ
- **B** 80 Ⓑ
- **C** 200 Ⓒ
- **D** 3200 Ⓓ

4 If $g(x) = 2x^3 + 1$, then $g(-2)$ is

- **A** −63 Ⓐ
- **B** −15 Ⓑ
- **C** −11 Ⓒ
- **D** −17 Ⓓ

5 The diagram shows the weekly allowance received by children in a class.

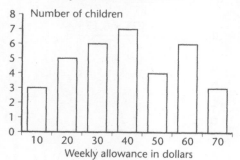

The mode of the distribution is

- **A** $30 Ⓐ
- **B** $40 Ⓑ
- **C** $50 Ⓒ
- **D** $60 Ⓓ

6 The diagonals of which of the following figures will always bisect each other and meet at right angles?

- **A** Rhombus Ⓐ
- **B** Rectangle Ⓑ
- **C** Parallelogram Ⓒ
- **D** Trapezium Ⓓ

7 A cylinder has a capacity of 88 cm³. Its volume in litres is

- **A** 0.088 Ⓐ
- **B** 0.88 Ⓑ
- **C** 8.8 Ⓒ
- **D** 88 Ⓓ

8 If $x = 2^2$, then x^3 is

- **A** 2 Ⓐ
- **B** 32 Ⓑ
- **C** 64 Ⓒ
- **D** 256 Ⓓ

9 Which of the following pairs of equations represents a pair of perpendicular lines?

- **A** $y = 6 + x, y = 6 + 2x$ Ⓐ
- **B** $y = 6 - 2x, y = 6 + x$ Ⓑ
- **C** $y = 6 + \frac{1}{2}x, y = 6 - 2x$ Ⓒ
- **D** $y = 6 - 2x, y = 3 - x$ Ⓓ

10

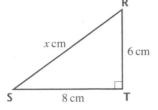

In the right-angled triangle STR, the sine of the angle RST is

A $\dfrac{6}{x}$ Ⓐ

B $\dfrac{8}{x}$ Ⓑ

C $\dfrac{6}{8}$ Ⓒ

D $\dfrac{x}{6}$ Ⓓ

11

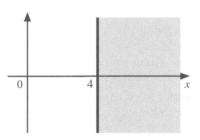

In the figure above, the shaded region represents

A $y \geq 4$ Ⓐ
B $x \leq 4$ Ⓑ
C $x \geq 4$ Ⓒ
D $y \leq 4$ Ⓓ

12   A square has an area of 900 cm². Its perimeter is

A   30 cm   Ⓐ
B   60 cm   Ⓑ
C   120 cm   Ⓒ
D   225 cm   Ⓓ

13   The simple interest on $1200 for 5 years at 4% per annum is

A $\$\dfrac{100 \times 4}{1200 \times 5}$ Ⓐ

B $\$\dfrac{1200 \times 5}{100 \times 4}$ Ⓑ

C $\$\dfrac{100 \times 5 \times 4}{1200}$ Ⓒ

D $\$\dfrac{1200 \times 4 \times 5}{100}$ Ⓓ

14   The number of kilograms in one thousandth of a tonne is

A   0.001   Ⓐ
B   0.01   Ⓑ
C   1   Ⓒ
D   1000   Ⓓ

15 $\dfrac{-(6x - 9y + 12)}{-3} =$

A $2x + 3y - 4$ Ⓐ
B $2x - 3y + 4$ Ⓑ
C $-2x - 3y - 4$ Ⓒ
D $-2x - 3y + 4$ Ⓓ

16   The mean of 100 scores in a distribution is 84. If each score in the distribution is increased by 2, the new mean of the distribution is

A   186   Ⓐ
B   184   Ⓑ
C   86   Ⓒ
D   42   Ⓓ

17   Given $\dfrac{12.3 \times 1.75}{6.15} = 3.5$,

the value of $\dfrac{123 \times 0.175}{6.15}$ is

A   0.35   Ⓐ
B   3.5   Ⓑ
C   35   Ⓒ
D   350   Ⓓ

18 $5x - 2y - 3(x - y) =$

  A $2x + y$ Ⓐ
  B $2x - 5y$ Ⓑ
  C $8x + y$ Ⓒ
  D $8x - 5y$ Ⓓ

19 The line graph which illustrates
$\{x: -4 < x \le 3\}$ is

A 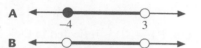   Ⓐ

B   Ⓑ
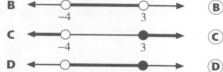
C   Ⓒ

D   Ⓓ

20 Which of the following numbers is prime?

  A   250   Ⓐ
  B   256   Ⓑ
  C   257   Ⓒ
  D   261   Ⓓ

21 Which of the following is the best
approximation to $\sqrt{630}$?

  A 2.51×10 Ⓐ
  B 2.51×10^2 Ⓑ
  C 7.94×10 Ⓒ
  D 7.94×10^2 Ⓓ

22

The histogram above shows the scores
obtained by students in a mathematics test
marked out of 7. The number of students
who sat the test is

  A   25   Ⓐ
  B   100   Ⓑ
  C   110   Ⓒ
  D   175   Ⓓ

23 The volume of a cube is $216\,\text{cm}^3$. Its total
surface area is

  A $6\,\text{cm}^2$ Ⓐ
  B $36\,\text{cm}^2$ Ⓑ
  C $144\,\text{cm}^2$ Ⓒ
  D $216\,\text{cm}^2$ Ⓓ

24 $8\frac{2}{3}\%$ of $600.00 is

  A $ 5.20   Ⓐ
  B $ 8.66   Ⓑ
  C $ 52.00   Ⓒ
  D $ 86.67   Ⓓ

25 If $1120.00 is shared in the ratio of $2 : 3 : 9$,
then the difference between the smallest
and largest shares is

  A $160.00   Ⓐ
  B $480.00   Ⓑ
  C $560.00   Ⓒ
  D $720.00   Ⓓ

26 A man buys a pair of trousers at a sale and
pays $120.00, saving $30.00 on the marked
price. The percentage discount is

  A   20   Ⓐ
  B   25   Ⓑ
  C $33\frac{1}{3}$ Ⓒ
  D   80   Ⓓ

27 The next term in the sequence
2, 6, 12, 20, … is

  A   24   Ⓐ
  B   28   Ⓑ
  C   30   Ⓒ
  D   40   Ⓓ

28 A salesman receives $101.00 commission
on his sales of $2020.00. This represents a
percentage of his sales of

  A   1%   Ⓐ
  B   2%   Ⓑ
  C   5%   Ⓒ
  D   20%   Ⓓ

29 If $a * b = a^b$, then $2 * 5 =$

A   10   Ⓐ
B   25   Ⓑ
C   32   Ⓒ
D   52   Ⓓ

30 A plane leaves town P at 09:15 hrs and arrives at town Q $4\frac{1}{2}$ hours later. At Q it is refuelled for 45 minutes and then travels for 2 hours before reaching town R. The time of arrival at R is

A   10:00 hrs   Ⓐ
B   13:45 hrs   Ⓑ
C   14:30 hrs   Ⓒ
D   16:30 hrs   Ⓓ

31 $A = \{p, q, m, n\}$, $B = \{p, q, t\}$, then $A \cap B$ is

A $\{p, q, m, n, t\}$ Ⓐ
B $\{p, q, m, n\}$ Ⓑ
C $\{p, q, m\}$ Ⓒ
D $\{p, q,\}$ Ⓓ

32 A rectangle has a length 9 metres and a width 5 metres, each measurement taken to the nearest metre. The range of possible values of its perimeter is

A   13 m to 15 m   Ⓐ
B   24 m to 32 m   Ⓑ
C   26 m to 30 m   Ⓒ
D   27 m to 29 m   Ⓓ

33 If $a = -4$, $b = -3$, then $a \times b =$

A -43 Ⓐ
B -12 Ⓑ
C 12 Ⓒ
D 43 Ⓓ

34 The area of the trapezium shown on the right is

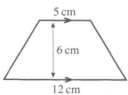

5 cm
6 cm
12 cm

A $60 \, \text{cm}^2$ Ⓐ
B $51 \, \text{cm}^2$ Ⓑ
C $23 \, \text{cm}^2$ Ⓒ
D $17 \, \text{cm}^2$ Ⓓ

35 Given that y varies inversely as the square root of x. If k is the constant of proportionality, then $y =$

A $\dfrac{k}{\sqrt{x}}$ Ⓐ

B $\dfrac{k}{x^2}$ Ⓑ

C kx^2 Ⓒ

D $k\sqrt{x}$ Ⓓ

36 The point P $(-4, 2)$ is reflected in the y-axis. The coordinates of its image will be

A $(4, 2)$ Ⓐ
B $(4, -2)$ Ⓑ
C $(-4, -2)$ Ⓒ
D $(2, -4)$ Ⓓ

37 The line $y = 3x - 12$ cuts the y-axis at P. The coordinates of P are

A $(-12, 0)$ Ⓐ
B $(-4, 0)$ Ⓑ
C $(0, -12)$ Ⓒ
D $(4, 0)$ Ⓓ

38 A pen costs $76.00 after a 5% discount is given off the marked price. The marked price is

A $79.80   Ⓐ
B $80.00   Ⓑ
C $81.00   Ⓒ
D $96.00   Ⓓ

39 The table below refers to the number of litres of milk given by cows on a farm.

Number of litres per day	11	12	13	14	15	16
Number of cows	6	3	5	4	4	3

The probability that a cow, chosen at random, gives at least 13 litres of milk is

A $\dfrac{5}{25}$ Ⓐ

B $\dfrac{11}{25}$ Ⓑ

C $\dfrac{14}{25}$ Ⓒ

D $\dfrac{16}{25}$ Ⓓ

40 An odd number, x, is added to an even number, y. The resulting sum, $x + y$, is always

A composite Ⓐ
B prime Ⓑ
C even Ⓒ
D odd Ⓓ

41 A washing machine was sold for $770.00 making a profit of 10%. The cost price was

A $77.00 Ⓐ
B $693.00 Ⓑ
C $700.00 Ⓒ
D $847.00 Ⓓ

42 A van was bought for $75 000.00 and depreciates by 10% each year. Its value after 2 years is

A $60 000.00 Ⓐ
B $60 750.00 Ⓑ
C $67 500.00 Ⓒ
D $68 250.00 Ⓓ

43 It is given that a set P is a proper subset of another set Q. If n is the number of elements in Q that are not in P then

A $n \geq 1$ Ⓐ
B $n > 1$ Ⓑ
C $n = 1$ Ⓒ
D $n = 0$ Ⓓ

44

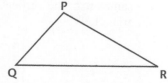

In triangle PQR, PQ < PR < QR. Which of the following is true about $\angle R$, $\angle Q$, and $\angle R$?

A $\angle P < \angle Q < \angle R$ Ⓐ
B $\angle P > \angle Q > \angle R$ Ⓑ
C $\angle Q < \angle P < \angle R$ Ⓒ
D $\angle Q > \angle P > \angle R$ Ⓓ

45 A mother is twice as old as her daughter. Ten years ago the mother was $(3x - 5)$ years old. The present age of the daughter is

A $\dfrac{3x + 5}{2}$ Ⓐ

B $\dfrac{3x - 5}{2}$ Ⓑ

C $\dfrac{3x + 5}{10}$ Ⓒ

D $\dfrac{3x - 5}{10}$ Ⓓ

46

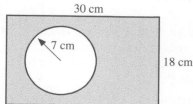

The diagram shows a circle of radius 7 cm within a rectangle of sides 30 cm and 18 cm. The area of the shaded region is

A 540 cm^2 Ⓐ
B 386 cm^2 Ⓑ
C 253 cm^2 Ⓒ
D 64 cm^2 Ⓓ

47 A man bought a watch for $240.00 and sold it to gain 20%. His gain was

A $48.00 Ⓐ
B $192.00 Ⓑ
C $260.00 Ⓒ
D $288.00 Ⓓ

48 The radius of the circle on the right is 21 cm. The length of the minor arc AB is

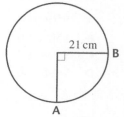

A 21 cm Ⓐ
B 33 cm Ⓑ
C 99 cm Ⓒ
D 132 cm Ⓓ

49 The sum of the interior angles of a hexagon is

- **A** 360°   Ⓐ
- **B** 480°   Ⓑ
- **C** 540°   Ⓒ
- **D** 720°   Ⓓ

50

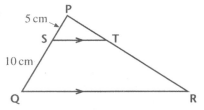

In triangle PQR, PS = 5 cm and SQ = 10 cm. If the area of the triangle PST = 12 cm^2 and ST is parallel to QR then the area of the triangle PQR is

- **A** 108 cm^2 Ⓐ
- **B** 96 cm^2 Ⓑ
- **C** 48 cm^2 Ⓒ
- **D** 24 cm^2 Ⓓ

51 $f(x) = 3x - 1$ and $g(x) = x^3$ then $fg(2) =$

- **A** 5   Ⓐ
- **B** 23   Ⓑ
- **C** 40   Ⓒ
- **D** 125   Ⓓ

52 A teacher receives $6000.00 in government bonds and accepts a cash trade at a bank of 83% of its face value. If the bank then charges a $23.00 service charge, then the cash received is

- **A** $6060.00   Ⓐ
- **B** $5003.00   Ⓑ
- **C** $4980.00   Ⓒ
- **D** $4957.00   Ⓓ

53 Given $S = \{$sports cars$\}$
$R = \{$red sports cars$\}$
This information can best be illustrated on a Venn diagram by:

A
U
R   S
          Ⓐ

B
U
R, S
          Ⓑ

C
U
S
R
          Ⓒ

D
U
R
S
          Ⓓ

54

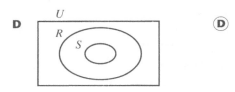

The triangle and the rectangle, shown above, have the same area. The vertical height, h, of the triangle is

- **A** 192 cm   Ⓐ
- **B** 144 cm   Ⓑ
- **C** 32 cm   Ⓒ
- **D** 16 cm   Ⓓ

55 26_{10} written in binary form is

- **A** 11010_2 Ⓐ
- **B** 10100_2 Ⓑ
- **C** 10011_2 Ⓒ
- **D** 10101_2 Ⓓ

56 On a particular day the probability that it rains is $\frac{2}{7}$ and the probability that a man wears a black suit is $\frac{3}{5}$. The probability that it does not rain and the man does not wear a black suit is

A $\frac{4}{35}$ Ⓐ

B $\frac{6}{35}$ Ⓑ

C $\frac{2}{7}$ Ⓒ

D $\frac{3}{7}$ Ⓓ

57 A certain quantity, x, is trebled and then diminished by three, resulting in seven. This statement may be expressed as

A $\frac{x^3}{3} = 7$ Ⓐ

B $3x - 3 = 7$ Ⓑ

C $3x + 3 = 7$ Ⓒ

D $\frac{3x - 3}{7} = 0$ Ⓓ

58

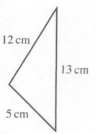

The above figure, not drawn to scale, shows a triangle with sides of 5 cm, 12 cm and 13 cm. The following statements have been made:

I   The triangle is acute angled.
II The triangle is right angled.
III The triangle is obtuse angled.
IV The triangle is scalene.

The correct statements are

A I and IV only Ⓐ
B I and III only Ⓑ
C II and III only Ⓒ
D II and IV only Ⓓ

59

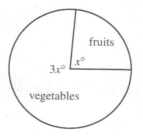

The pie chart above shows the size of the angles representing vegetables and fruits grown on a farm. The percentage of the land allocated to vegetables is

A 75% Ⓐ
B 50% Ⓑ
C $33\frac{1}{3}$% Ⓒ
D 25% Ⓓ

60

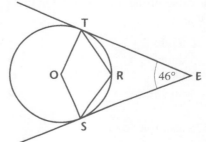

The tangents at T and S to a circle, centre O, meet at E. R is a point on the circumference and ∠TES = 46°. The size of ∠TRS is

A 134° Ⓐ
B 113° Ⓑ
C 90° Ⓒ
D 67° Ⓓ

Test number ❷

Read the directions on page (iv) carefully.

1 The graph most suitable to display the daily maximum temperature of an island is

A	pie chart	Ⓐ
B	bar chart	Ⓑ
C	line graph	Ⓒ
D	histogram	Ⓓ

2 The value of the digit 5 in the number 4536.3 is

A	5 tenths	Ⓐ
B	5 units	Ⓑ
C	5 tens	Ⓒ
D	5 hundreds	Ⓓ

3 0.375 as a fraction is

A	$\frac{1}{2}$	Ⓐ
B	$\frac{3}{8}$	Ⓑ
C	$\frac{1}{4}$	Ⓒ
D	$\frac{1}{8}$	Ⓓ

4 A ship is sailing on a bearing of 090°. Its direction is

A	East	Ⓐ
B	West	Ⓑ
C	North	Ⓒ
D	South	Ⓓ

5 0.062 written in standard form is

A	6.2×10^3	Ⓐ
B	6.2×10^2	Ⓑ
C	6.2×10^{-2}	Ⓒ
D	6.2×10^{-3}	Ⓓ

6

In the triangle above, the value of $2x$ is

A	30°	Ⓐ
B	60°	Ⓑ
C	90°	Ⓒ
D	180°	Ⓓ

7 If $R = \{$rectangles$\}$ and $P = \{$parallelograms$\}$, then

A	$R \subset P$	Ⓐ
B	$P \subset R$	Ⓑ
C	$P = R$	Ⓒ
D	$P \cap R = \varnothing$	Ⓓ

8 The smallest positive integer x, such that $x > \sqrt{20}$ is

A	25	Ⓐ
B	21	Ⓑ
C	5	Ⓒ
D	4	Ⓓ

9 The positive value of $\sqrt[4]{16}$ is

A	2	Ⓐ
B	4	Ⓑ
C	8	Ⓒ
D	64	Ⓓ

Questions 10–12 are based on the table given below.

The following marks were obtained by 20 students in a test

Mark	1	2	3	4	5
Number of students	2	3	4	8	3

10 The modal mark is

A 8 Ⓐ
B 5 Ⓑ
C 4 Ⓒ
D 3 Ⓓ

11 The mean mark is

A 0.75 Ⓐ
B 3.35 Ⓑ
C 10 Ⓒ
D 15 Ⓓ

12 The median mark is

A 2 Ⓐ
B 3 Ⓑ
C 4 Ⓒ
D 5 Ⓓ

13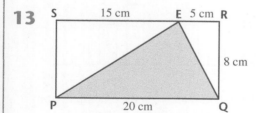

E is a point on the side SR of rectangle PQRS. If PQ is 20 cm and QR is 8 cm then the area of triangle PQE is

A $\dfrac{20 \times 8}{2}$ cm^2 Ⓐ

B $\dfrac{20 \times 8}{3}$ cm^2 Ⓑ

C $\dfrac{20 \times 8}{4}$ cm^2 Ⓒ

D $\dfrac{20 \times 8}{5}$ cm^2 Ⓓ

14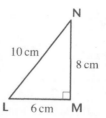

The value of tan ∠N in the triangle LMN is

A $\dfrac{6}{10}$ Ⓐ

B $\dfrac{6}{8}$ Ⓑ

C $\dfrac{8}{10}$ Ⓒ

D $\dfrac{8}{6}$ Ⓓ

15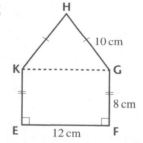

The perimeter of the shape EFGHK shown above is

A 72 cm Ⓐ
B 60 cm Ⓑ
C 48 cm Ⓒ
D 30 cm Ⓓ

16 $1.2 \times 1.2 \times 1.2 = 1.728$
The value of $1.2 \times 0.12 \times 12 =$

A 1728 Ⓐ
B 172.8 Ⓑ
C 17.28 Ⓒ
D 1.728 Ⓓ

17

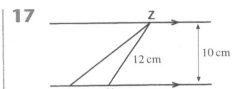

In the above figure the area of triangle XYZ is

A 30 cm²   Ⓐ

B 36 cm²   Ⓑ

C 60 cm²   Ⓒ

D 72 cm²   Ⓓ

18 $f(x) = 2x - 1$ $f^{-1}(x)$ is given by

A $\dfrac{(x+1)}{2}$ Ⓐ

B $2(x+1)$ Ⓑ

C $2(x-1)$ Ⓒ

D $\dfrac{(x-1)}{2}$ Ⓓ

19 If a and b are vectors such that $a = \begin{pmatrix} 2 \\ 1 \end{pmatrix}$, and $b = \begin{pmatrix} -3 \\ 2 \end{pmatrix}$ then $a - 2b$ is

A $\begin{pmatrix} -1 \\ 3 \end{pmatrix}$ Ⓐ

B $\begin{pmatrix} -4 \\ 5 \end{pmatrix}$ Ⓑ

C $\begin{pmatrix} 5 \\ -1 \end{pmatrix}$ Ⓒ

D $\begin{pmatrix} 8 \\ -3 \end{pmatrix}$ Ⓓ

20 A man travelled from P to Q in $13\frac{1}{4}$ hours. He left P at 13:15 hrs. His time of arrival at Q was

A 24:00 hrs   Ⓐ

B 13:15 hrs   Ⓑ

C 02:30 hrs   Ⓒ

D 00:00 hrs   Ⓓ

21 $5x - 2y - 3(2x - y) =$

A $11x + 5y$ Ⓐ

B $-x + y$ Ⓑ

C $-x - 5y$ Ⓒ

D $x - 5y$ Ⓓ

22 A line has gradient -2 and cuts the y-axis at $(0, 3)$. Its equation may be written as

A $y = 2x - 3$ Ⓐ

B $y = -2x + 3$ Ⓑ

C $y = -2x - 3$ Ⓒ

D $y = 2x + 3$ Ⓓ

23

x	1	2	3	4
$f(x)$	2	4	8	16

Which of the following represents the above table of values?

A $f : x \to 2x^2 - 1$ Ⓐ

B $f : x \to 3x - 2$ Ⓑ

C $f : x \to 2x + 1$ Ⓒ

D $f : x \to 2^x$ Ⓓ

24

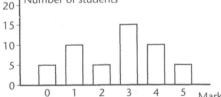

The diagram above shows the number of students and the marks obtained in a certain test. The number of students who sat the test was

A 15   Ⓐ

B 35   Ⓑ

C 50   Ⓒ

D 60   Ⓓ

25 The set of values of x such that x is greater than or equal to four but less than seven may be represented as

A $4 \leq x \leq 7$ Ⓐ
B $4 < x < 7$ Ⓑ
C $4 < x \leq 7$ Ⓒ
D $4 \leq x < 7$ Ⓓ

26 $3^x \div 3^{-y} =$

A 3^{x+y} Ⓐ
B 3^{x-y} Ⓑ
C 3^{xy} Ⓒ
D 3^{-xy} Ⓓ

27   The matrix $\begin{pmatrix} 2 & 0 \\ 0 & 2 \end{pmatrix}$ represents

A   reflection in the line $y = x$ Ⓐ
B   reflection in x-axis   Ⓑ
C   rotation about O, through 180°   Ⓒ
D   enlargement, about O, and scale factor 2   Ⓓ

28

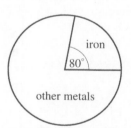

The pie-chart above represents the mass of metals in an alloy. The percentage of iron in the alloy is

A   80%   Ⓐ
B $77\frac{7}{9}\%$ Ⓑ
C $22\frac{2}{9}\%$ Ⓒ
D   10%   Ⓓ

29   If $v^2 = u^2 + 2as$, then

A $s = \dfrac{v^2 + u^2}{2a}$ Ⓐ

B $s = \dfrac{v^2 - u^2}{2a}$ Ⓑ

C $s = \dfrac{2a}{v^2 + u^2}$ Ⓒ

D $s = \dfrac{2a}{v^2 - u^2}$ Ⓓ

30   A square field has an area of 144 m². Its perimeter is

A   6 m   Ⓐ
B   24 m   Ⓑ
C   36 m   Ⓒ
D   48 m   Ⓓ

31   A mixture consists of 3 parts of an element P, 2 parts of an element Q and 4 parts of an element R. In 99 kg of the mixture, the amount of the element Q is

A   1 kg   Ⓐ
B   22 kg   Ⓑ
C   33 kg   Ⓒ
D   44 kg   Ⓓ

32   If $g(x) = 3x + 4$, then $g^{-1}(x)$ is

A $\dfrac{(x - 4)}{3}$ Ⓐ

B $\dfrac{(3x - 4)}{3}$ Ⓑ

C $\dfrac{(x + 4)}{3}$ Ⓒ

D $\dfrac{(3x + 4)}{3}$ Ⓓ

33   The number of square metres in one hectare is

A   1 000   Ⓐ
B   10 000   Ⓑ
C   100 000   Ⓒ
D   1 000 000   Ⓓ

34 The marked price of an electronic calculator is $150.00. If a 10% discount is given and there is a 15% sales tax, then a buyer would pay

   A $155.25   Ⓐ
   B $157.50   Ⓑ
   C $172.50   Ⓒ
   D $189.75   Ⓓ

35 The simple interest on $100.00 in 32 years amounted to $160. The rate of interest per annum was

   A   1.6%   Ⓐ
   B   3.125%   Ⓑ
   C   5%   Ⓒ
   D   8%   Ⓓ

36 $2(3a - 2b) - 4(2a - 3b) =$

   A $-2a - 16b$ Ⓐ
   B $-2a - 8b$ Ⓑ
   C $-2a + 8b$ Ⓒ
   D $2a + 8b$ Ⓓ

37 If $4x^2 + ax + 25$ is a perfect square then the possible values of a are

   A   4, 25   Ⓐ
   B $6\frac{1}{4}, -6\frac{1}{4}$ Ⓑ
   C   16, 625   Ⓒ
   D   20, −20   Ⓓ

38

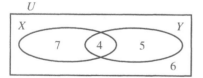

The number of elements in $(X \cup Y)'$ is

   A   22   Ⓐ
   B   16   Ⓑ
   C   12   Ⓒ
   D   6   Ⓓ

39

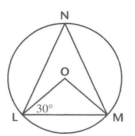

In the figure above (not drawn to scale), O is the centre of the circle and L, M and N are points on the circumference.
$\angle LNM =$

   A   120°   Ⓐ
   B   90°   Ⓑ
   C   60°   Ⓒ
   D   30°   Ⓓ

40

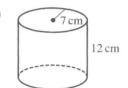

The figure above shows a solid, right cylinder of radius 7 cm and height 12 cm. The total surface area is

   A $266\pi \, \text{cm}^2$ Ⓐ
   B $217\pi \, \text{cm}^2$ Ⓑ
   C $98\pi \, \text{cm}^2$ Ⓒ
   D $84\pi \, \text{cm}^2$ Ⓓ

41 A line $2y = 6x + 1$ has a perpendicular line drawn through it. The gradient of this perpendicular line is

   A   −6   Ⓐ
   B   +3   Ⓑ
   C $-\frac{1}{3}$ Ⓒ
   D $-\frac{1}{6}$ Ⓓ

42 Three light bulbs are switched on simultaneously and flash at intervals of 2, 5 and 10 seconds respectively. They will flash together for the first time after

A   10 s   Ⓐ
B   20 s   Ⓑ
C   50 s   Ⓒ
D   100 s   Ⓓ

43 Which of the following figures represent functions?

(i)

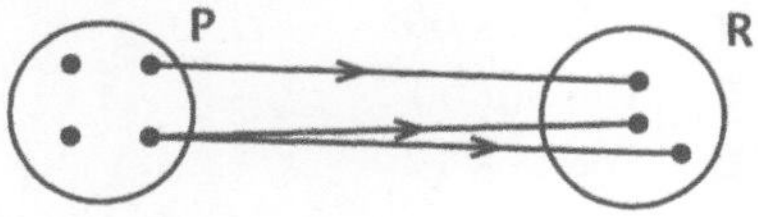

(ii)

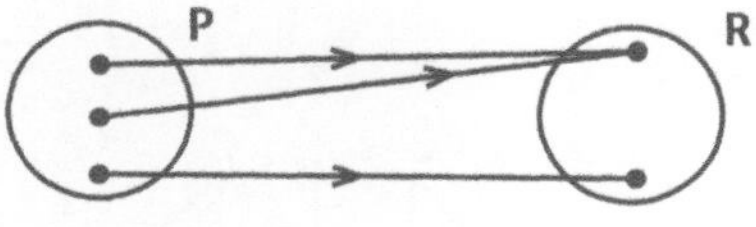

(iii)

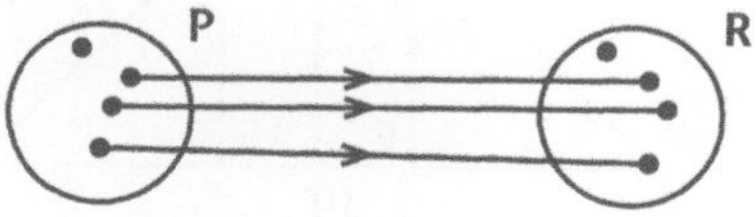

(iv)

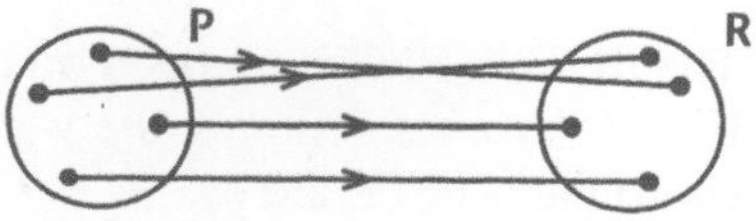

A   (i), (ii), (iii), (iv)   Ⓐ
B   (ii) and (iv) only   Ⓑ
C   (ii), (iii) and (iv)   Ⓒ
D   (ii) and (iii) only   Ⓓ

44 Before a sale the price of a shirt was marked up by 20% from $80.00. At the sale there was a discount of 20%. The sale price of the shirt was

A $96.00   Ⓐ
B $80.00   Ⓑ
C $76.80   Ⓒ
D $64.00   Ⓓ

45 The missing term in the series $7\frac{1}{3}$, *, 6, and $5\frac{1}{3}$, is

A $7\frac{2}{3}$ Ⓐ
B   7   Ⓑ
C $6\frac{2}{3}$ Ⓒ
D $6\frac{1}{3}$ Ⓓ

46 Given that y varies as the square of x and inversely as the square root of z, then y is proportional to

A $x^2\sqrt{z}$ Ⓐ

B $(\sqrt{x})z^2$ Ⓑ

C $\dfrac{\sqrt{x}}{z^2}$ Ⓒ

D $\dfrac{x^2}{\sqrt{z}}$ Ⓓ

47

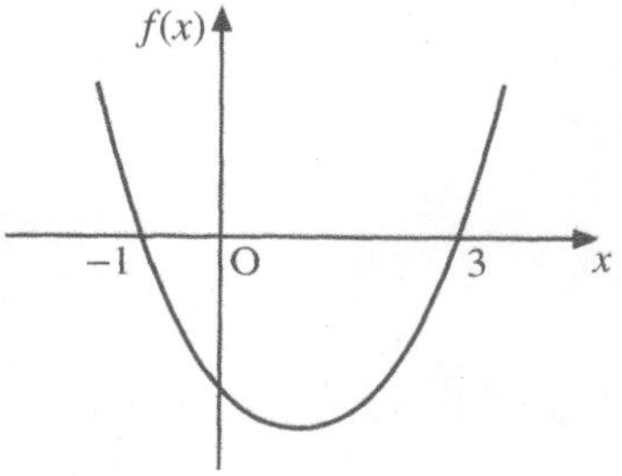

From the graph the values for which $f(x)$ is negative will be

A $-1 < x \le 3$ Ⓐ
B $-1 \le x < 3$ Ⓑ
C $-1 < x < 3$ Ⓒ
D $-1 \le x \le 3$ Ⓓ

48 The lines $y = 3x + 1$ and $2y - 6x + 1 = 0$

A   are perpendicular   Ⓐ
B   are parallel   Ⓑ
C   pass through the origin   Ⓒ
D   cut the y-axis at the same point   Ⓓ

49

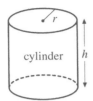

The figures above show a right circular cylinder of base radius r and height h and a cone of base radius r and height H.
If the figures above have the same volume then which of the following is true?

A $h = \frac{1}{3}H$ Ⓐ

B $H = \frac{1}{3}h$ Ⓑ

C $h = H$ Ⓒ

D $h^2 = \frac{1}{3}H^2$ Ⓓ

50 The interior angles of a pentagon are $3x°$, $2x°$, $2x°$, $2x°$ and $x°$. The size of the largest angle is

A   540° Ⓐ

B   162° Ⓑ

C   54° Ⓒ

D   36° Ⓓ

51 S and T are 2 finite sets such that $n(S) = n(T) = 9$. If $n(S \cup T) = 15$, then $n(S \cap T)$ is

A   1 Ⓐ

B   3 Ⓑ

C   6 Ⓒ

D   7 Ⓓ

52 $a^2 - (b + c)^2$ may be expressed as

A $(a - b - c)^2$ Ⓐ

B $(a - b + c)(a + b + c)$ Ⓑ

C $(a - b + c)(a + b - c)$ Ⓒ

D $(a - b - c)(a + b + c)$ Ⓓ

53

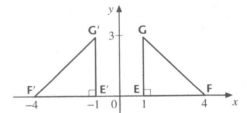

The diagram shows a parallelogram PQRS with sides QP = 12 cm, QR = 18 cm and angle PQR = 60°. The area of the triangle QRS, in cm², is

A   216 sin 60° Ⓐ

B   108 cos 60° Ⓑ

C   108 sin 60° Ⓒ

D   108 cos 120° Ⓓ

54

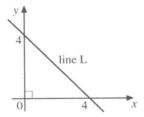

The triangle EFG is mapped on to triangle E′F′G′ by a reflection in the y-axis. The coordinates of G′ are

A $(-1, -3)$ Ⓐ

B $(-1, 3)$ Ⓑ

C $(1, -3)$ Ⓒ

D $(1, 3)$ Ⓓ

55

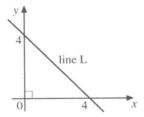

The equation of the line, L, is

A $y = \frac{1}{4}x$ Ⓐ

B $y = 4x$ Ⓑ

C $y = x + 4$ Ⓒ

D $y + x = 4$ Ⓓ

56 Cos 120° has the same value as

A   −cos 60°   Ⓐ
B   cos 60°   Ⓑ
C   sin 60°   Ⓒ
D   −sin 60°   Ⓓ

57

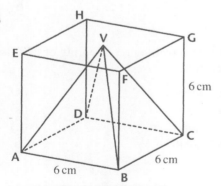

In the triangle above the following statements were made

I $\cos x° = \sin (90° − x°)$
II $b^2 = a^2 + c^2$
III $\sin x° = \cos (90° − x°)$
IV $\tan x° = \dfrac{b}{a}$

The correct statements are

A   I and II only   Ⓐ
B   II and IV only   Ⓑ
C   I and III only   Ⓒ
D   I, II and IV only   Ⓓ

58

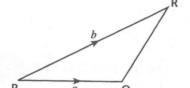

The pyramid VABCD has the same base and vertical height as the cube ABCDEFGH of side 6 cm. The volume of the pyramid is

A   216 cm³   Ⓐ
B   108 cm³   Ⓑ
C   72 cm³   Ⓒ
D   54 cm³   Ⓓ

59

If $\overrightarrow{PQ} = a$ and $\overrightarrow{PR} = b$, then the vector represented by $\overrightarrow{QR}$ in terms of a and b is

A $a − b$ Ⓐ
B $−a + b$ Ⓑ
C $−a − b$ Ⓒ
D $a + b$ Ⓓ

60 A bag contains three times as many blue marbles as red. If 12 red marbles are added to the bag, the probability of choosing a red or a blue marble is the same. The number of blue marbles in the bag is

A   48   Ⓐ
B   36   Ⓑ
C   18   Ⓒ
D   6   Ⓓ

Test number ③

Read the directions on page (iv) carefully.

1 $2^{12} \div 2^{-3} =$

   A 2^{-4} Ⓐ

   B 2^{4} Ⓑ

   C 2^{9} Ⓒ

   D 2^{15} Ⓓ

2   What percentage of 36 is 24?

   A 24% Ⓐ

   B $33\frac{1}{3}\%$ Ⓑ

   C $66\frac{2}{3}\%$ Ⓒ

   D 150% Ⓓ

3   If a and b are two integers, such that $a > b$, then $\sqrt{a^2 - b^2}$ means

   A   the square root of the difference of their squares   Ⓐ

   B   the square root of their difference, to be squared   Ⓑ

   C   the square root of their difference squared   Ⓒ

   D   the square of the root of their difference   Ⓓ

4   If x is a positive even number, then $x + 2$ will be

   A   odd   Ⓐ

   B   even   Ⓑ

   C   prime   Ⓒ

   D   negative   Ⓓ

5   A book was bought for \$99.00. What was the selling price if it was sold at a profit of 32%?

   A   \$31.68   Ⓐ

   B   \$67.32   Ⓑ

   C   \$75.00   Ⓒ

   D   \$130.68   Ⓓ

6 $\dfrac{9xy^2 + 12y}{81y}$ reduced to its lowest terms is

   A $\dfrac{9xy^2 + 4}{27}$ Ⓐ

   B $\dfrac{xy + 4}{9}$ Ⓑ

   C $\dfrac{3xy + 4}{27}$ Ⓒ

   D $\dfrac{xy + 12y}{9}$ Ⓓ

7   A ship travelling on a bearing of 270° is travelling

   A   west   Ⓐ

   B   east   Ⓑ

   C   north   Ⓒ

   D   south   Ⓓ

8

The diagram above illustrates the set of numbers x such that

   A $x \le 5$ Ⓐ

   B $x \ge 5$ Ⓑ

   C $x > 5$ Ⓒ

   D $x < 5$ Ⓓ

9 At a sale a dress costing $60.00 is given a 20% discount. The saving is

- A $72.00 Ⓐ
- B $50.00 Ⓑ
- C $48.00 Ⓒ
- D $12.00 Ⓓ

10 $3\frac{1}{8}$ in decimal form is

- A 31.25 Ⓐ
- B 3.125 Ⓑ
- C 0.3125 Ⓒ
- D 0.03125 Ⓓ

11 If $a * b$ denotes b^a, then $2 * 3$ is

- A 8 Ⓐ
- B 9 Ⓑ
- C 23 Ⓒ
- D 32 Ⓓ

12 $(2x + 1)(3 - 2x)$ may be written as

- A $3 - 4x - 4x^2$ Ⓐ
- B $3 - 4x + 4x^2$ Ⓑ
- C $3 + 4x - 4x^2$ Ⓒ
- D $3 + 4x + 4x^2$ Ⓓ

13

The diagram represents the mapping

- A $f : x \rightarrow 3x^2$ Ⓐ
- B $f : x \rightarrow 3x$ Ⓑ
- C $f : x \rightarrow 3x^3$ Ⓒ
- D $f : x \rightarrow 3^x$ Ⓓ

14 The missing term in the series
$10, *, 8\frac{2}{3}, 8, 7\frac{1}{3}$ is

- A $8\frac{1}{3}$ Ⓐ
- B 9 Ⓑ
- C $9\frac{1}{3}$ Ⓒ
- D $9\frac{2}{3}$ Ⓓ

15 The total surface area of a cube of side 4 cm is

- A $12 \, cm^2$ Ⓐ
- B $24 \, cm^2$ Ⓑ
- C $64 \, cm^2$ Ⓒ
- D $96 \, cm^2$ Ⓓ

16 $2(3x - 5y) - 2(5y - 3x) =$

- A $12x - 20y$ Ⓐ
- B $-12x + 20y$ Ⓑ
- C 0 Ⓒ
- D $16x - 16y$ Ⓓ

17 If $P = \{p, q, r\}$ and $Q = (t, u, v\}$ then $n(P \cap Q)$ is

- A 0 Ⓐ
- B 3 Ⓑ
- C 6 Ⓒ
- D 8 Ⓓ

18 If $3\frac{1}{2} : 4\frac{1}{2} = 5\frac{1}{2} : x$, then $x =$

- A $6\frac{1}{2}$ Ⓐ
- B $7\frac{1}{14}$ Ⓑ
- C $7\frac{1}{2}$ Ⓒ
- D $14\frac{2}{7}$ Ⓓ

19 A loan of $16 000.00 was repaid in 4 years by monthly payments of $400.00. The total percentage interest charged on the loan was

- A 5% Ⓐ
- B $8\frac{1}{3}\%$ Ⓑ
- C $16\frac{2}{3}\%$ Ⓒ
- D 20% Ⓓ

20 $3.46 \times 10^{-2} =$

- A 0.003 46 Ⓐ
- B 0.034 6 Ⓑ
- C 34.6 Ⓒ
- D 346.0 Ⓓ

21 $f(x) = px - q$. If $f(0) = -1$ and $f(1) = 3$ then p is

- A   2   Ⓐ
- B   3   Ⓑ
- C   4   Ⓒ
- D   5   Ⓓ

22 Mark did $\frac{2}{5}$ of a job and Alan did $\frac{1}{3}$ of the remainder. The fraction of the job left undone is

- A $\frac{1}{15}$ Ⓐ
- B $\frac{4}{15}$ Ⓑ
- C $\frac{2}{5}$ Ⓒ
- D $\frac{3}{5}$ Ⓓ

23 Each year a vehicle depreciates by 5% of its value at the start of that year. If it was bought for $20 000, its value after 2 years will be

- A $15 000   Ⓐ
- B $18 000   Ⓑ
- C $18 050   Ⓒ
- D $22 000   Ⓓ

24 An imported item bought for $150.00, was then subject to
(i)   purchase tax – 20% of its cost
(ii) customs duty – 50% of its cost
The total cost of the item will be

- A $255.00   Ⓐ
- B $220.00   Ⓑ
- C $195.00   Ⓒ
- D $180.00   Ⓓ

25

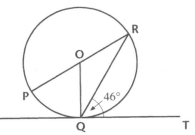

In the above diagram, not drawn to scale, POR is a diameter of a circle, centre O and QT is the tangent at Q. If $\angle RQT = 46°$, then $\angle ORQ$ is

- A   67°   Ⓐ
- B   46°   Ⓑ
- C   45°   Ⓒ
- D   44°   Ⓓ

26 $(0.01)^3 =$

- A   0.03   Ⓐ
- B   0.000 3   Ⓑ
- C   0.000 1   Ⓒ
- D   0.000 001   Ⓓ

27 The diameter of a circle with a circumference of 132 cm, in cm is $\left(\pi = \frac{22}{7}\right)$

- A $\sqrt{21}$ Ⓐ
- B $\sqrt{42}$ Ⓑ
- C   21   Ⓒ
- D   42   Ⓓ

28

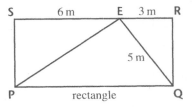

PQRS is a rectangle with E a point on SR such that SE = 6 m and ER = 3 m. Given that EQ is 5 m, the area of the rectangle is

- A $90\,\text{m}^2$ Ⓐ
- B $45\,\text{m}^2$ Ⓑ
- C $36\,\text{m}^2$ Ⓒ
- D $14\,\text{m}^2$ Ⓓ

29 Tom works at an hourly rate of $12.00. Allan receives one and a half times this rate. In a 40 hour week, Allan will receive

A $480.00   Ⓐ
B $720.00   Ⓑ
C $960.00   Ⓒ
D $1200.00   Ⓓ

30 The highest common factor of the set of numbers {54, 72, 90, 108} is

A   9   Ⓐ
B   18   Ⓑ
C   108   Ⓒ
D   1080   Ⓓ

31

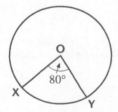

In the diagram, X and Y are points on the circumference of a circle, centre O.
If the circumference is 7.2 cm and angle XOY = 80°, then the length of the minor arc XY is

A   1.6 cm   Ⓐ
B   5.6 cm   Ⓑ
C   7.2 cm   Ⓒ
D   8.0 cm   Ⓓ

32 The length of a rectangle is halved and its width doubled. The area of the new rectangle is

A   doubled   Ⓐ
B   halved   Ⓑ
C   the same   Ⓒ
D   quartered   Ⓓ

33

In triangle STR, shown above, sin ∠TSR is

A $\frac{3}{4}$ Ⓐ
B $\frac{4}{5}$ Ⓑ
C $\frac{5}{6}$ Ⓒ
D $\frac{5}{4}$ Ⓓ

34

NPQ is a semi-circle attached to the side NQ of a rectangle MNQR, as shown in the diagram. MR = 14 m and RQ is 28 m. The perimeter of MNPQR is

A   92 m   Ⓐ
B   106 m   Ⓑ
C   114 m   Ⓒ
D   128 m   Ⓓ

35 The simple interest on $1600.00 for 3 years was $108.00. The rate percent was

A $\frac{4}{9}\%$ Ⓐ
B $2\frac{1}{4}\%$ Ⓑ
C   5%   Ⓒ
D   8%   Ⓓ

36

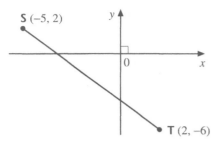

S (−5, 2)

T (2, −6)

The gradient of the line ST is

A $\frac{8}{7}$ Ⓐ

B $\frac{7}{8}$ Ⓑ

C $-\frac{7}{8}$ Ⓒ

D $-\frac{8}{7}$ Ⓓ

37

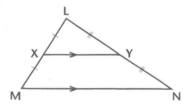

LMN is a triangle and X and Y are the midpoints of LM and LN respectively. If the area of triangle LXY is $9\,\text{cm}^2$ then the area of triangle LMN is

A $18\,\text{cm}^2$ Ⓐ

B $27\,\text{cm}^2$ Ⓑ

C $36\,\text{cm}^2$ Ⓒ

D $72\,\text{cm}^2$ Ⓓ

38

cube volume = $125\,\text{cm}^3$

The volume of the above cube is $125\,\text{cm}^3$. The area of each face is

A $5\,\text{cm}^2$ Ⓐ

B $10\,\text{cm}^2$ Ⓑ

C $25\,\text{cm}^2$ Ⓒ

D $60\,\text{cm}^2$ Ⓓ

39 Which pair of lines is parallel?

A $y = 2x - 3$ Ⓐ
   $y = -2x - 3$

B $y = 2 - 5x$ Ⓑ
   $y = -5x + 7$

C $y = \frac{1}{3}x + 2$ Ⓒ
   $y = -3x - 7$

D $y = x + 1$ Ⓓ
   $y = 2x + 2$

40 $G = \{a, b, c, d\}$. The number of subsets of G is

A 16   Ⓐ

B 8   Ⓑ

C 4   Ⓒ

D 0   Ⓓ

Questions 41–44 refer to the following table which shows the marks obtained by students in an examination.

Marks	0	1	2	3	4	5
Number of students	8	11	17	20	22	7

41 The number of students who wrote the test is

A 15   Ⓐ

B 22   Ⓑ

C 85   Ⓒ

D 100   Ⓓ

42 The mean mark to one decimal place is

A 2.7   Ⓐ

B 4   Ⓑ

C 5.5   Ⓒ

D 15   Ⓓ

43 The median mark of the distribution is

A 2   Ⓐ

B 3   Ⓑ

C 4   Ⓒ

D 6   Ⓓ

44 The probability that a student chosen at random attains a mark of 3 is

A $\frac{2}{17}$ Ⓐ

B $\frac{3}{17}$ Ⓑ

C $\frac{4}{17}$ Ⓒ

D $\frac{5}{17}$ Ⓓ

45 Given that y varies as the square of x, and y is 2 when x is 1, the value of y when $x = 2$ is

A 8 Ⓐ

B 6 Ⓑ

C 2 Ⓒ

D 1 Ⓓ

46 Which of the following sets of numbers could represent the sides of a right angled triangle?

A {4, 6, 8} Ⓐ

B {5, 12, 13} Ⓑ

C {6, 8, 12} Ⓒ

D {7, 10, 15} Ⓓ

47 The point H (a, b) is translated by a vector $\begin{pmatrix} -2 \\ 1 \end{pmatrix}$ to a point H′. The coordinates of H′ are

A $(a+2, b-1)$ Ⓐ

B $(a-2, b-1)$. Ⓑ

C $(a+2, b+1)$ Ⓒ

D $(a-2, b+1)$ Ⓓ

48 0.008×25 in standard form is

A 2×10^{-2} Ⓐ

B 2×10^{-1} Ⓑ

C 2×10^{2} Ⓒ

D 2×10^{3} Ⓓ

49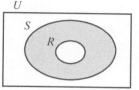

In the Venn diagram above, the shaded region represents

A $(R \cup S)'$ Ⓐ

B $(R \cap S)'$ Ⓑ

C $R \cap S'$ Ⓒ

D $R' \cap S$ Ⓓ

50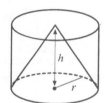

A cone is inscribed in a cylinder so that they have the same base of radius r, and vertical height h. The ratio of the volume of the cylinder to the volume of the cone is

A $1:2$ Ⓐ

B $1:3$ Ⓑ

C $2:1$ Ⓒ

D $3:1$ Ⓓ

51 A rectangle is twice as long as it is wide. If its width is w cm, then its perimeter is

A $8w^{2}$ cm Ⓐ

B $2w^{2}$ cm Ⓑ

C $6w$ cm Ⓒ

D $2w$ cm Ⓓ

52 The median of the set of numbers
7, 1, 8, 3, 6, 2 is

  A $4\frac{1}{2}$ Ⓐ

  B   5   Ⓑ

  C $5\frac{1}{2}$ Ⓒ

  D   9   Ⓓ

53 Which of the following is not a rational
number?

  A $\sqrt{9}$ Ⓐ

  B $\sqrt{12}$ Ⓑ

  C $\sqrt{16}$ Ⓒ

  D $\sqrt{36}$ Ⓓ

54 If A has \$$x$ and B has twice as much as C
who has 3 times as much as A, then B has

  A   \$$2x$ Ⓐ

  B   \$$3x$ Ⓑ

  C   \$$6x$ Ⓒ

  D   \$$10x$ Ⓓ

55 Another name for a cumulative frequency
graph is

  A   upper quartile   Ⓐ

  B   ogive   Ⓑ

  C   inter-quartile range   Ⓒ

  D   frequency curve   Ⓓ

56

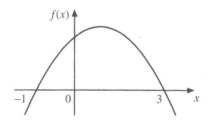

The set of values for which $f(x) > 0$ is

  A $-1 \le x < 3$ Ⓐ

  B $-1 < x \le 3$ Ⓑ

  C $-1 < x < 3$ Ⓒ

  D $-1 \le x \le 3$ Ⓓ

57

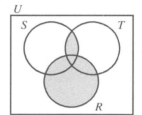

In the figure above PQ and RS are parallel
lines cut by the transversal XY. The value
of x is

  A   120°   Ⓐ

  B   90°   Ⓑ

  C   60°   Ⓒ

  D   30°   Ⓓ

58

In the Venn diagram, shown above, the
shaded region represents

  A $(S \cup T) \cap R$ Ⓐ

  B $(S \cap T) \cup R$ Ⓑ

  C $(S \cap R) \cup T$ Ⓒ

  D $(S \cap T) \cap R$ Ⓓ

59 The point (2, 5) is rotated through 90° about
O to a point P. The coordinates of P are

  A $(-5, 2)$ Ⓐ

  B $(5, 2)$ Ⓑ

  C $(5, -2)$ Ⓒ

  D $(-5, -2)$ Ⓓ

60 If $x^2 + kx + 9$ is a perfect square then k
could be

  A   3   Ⓐ

  B   6, or −6   Ⓑ

  C   36, or −36   Ⓒ

  D   81   Ⓓ

Test number 4

Read the directions on page (iv) carefully.

1 $2^6 \div 2^{-2} =$

   A 2^{-3} (A)

   B 2^{-12} (B)

   C 2^6 (C)

   D 2^8 (D)

2 $3(a^2b^2)^2 =$

   A $3a^4b^5$ (A)

   B $9a^4b^6$ (B)

   C $3a^4b^4$ (C)

   D $9a^4b^9$ (D)

3   The simple interest obtained on $14 000.00 borrowed at the rate of 5% per annum, for 3 years, is

   A $210.00   (A)

   B $420.00   (B)

   C $740.00   (C)

   D $2100.00   (D)

4   A table with a marked price of $200.00 was given a discount of 10% at a sale. The sale price was

   A $200.00   (A)

   B $210.00   (B)

   C $190.00   (C)

   D $180.00   (D)

5

The number line above indicates the values of x such that

   A $x \le -3$ (A)

   B $x < -3$ (B)

   C $x > -3$ (C)

   D $x \ge -3$ (D)

6   4.60 as a mixed fraction is

   A $\frac{46}{100}$ (A)

   B $4\frac{3}{5}$ (B)

   C $6\frac{4}{10}$ (C)

   D $6\frac{2}{5}$ (D)

7

The above diagram illustrates the mapping of elements of set R onto elements of set T. The mapping is not a function because

   A   no element in R is mapped to s in T (A)

   B   there are only 4 elements in R and 4 elements in T (B)

   C $d \in R$ is not mapped on to any element in T (C)

   D   only one arrow leaves each element in R (D)

8   For the object and image to be congruent in an enlargement, the scale factor, k, has to be

   A $k < 1$ (A)

   B $k > 1$ (B)

   C $k = 1$ (C)

   D $k = 0$ (D)

9 0.625 is equivalent to

A $\frac{1}{4}$ Ⓐ

B $\frac{3}{8}$ Ⓑ

C $\frac{1}{2}$ Ⓒ

D $\frac{5}{8}$ Ⓓ

10 5 tonnes, expressed in kilograms is

A 5000   Ⓐ

B 500   Ⓑ

C 50   Ⓒ

D $\frac{5}{1000}$ Ⓓ

11 A cube of side 3 cm, has a volume of

A $27\,cm^3$ Ⓐ

B $36\,cm^3$ Ⓑ

C $54\,cm^3$ Ⓒ

D $51\,cm^3$ Ⓓ

12 The number property shown in the statement $3(2 + 7) = (3 \times 2) + (3 \times 7)$ is the

A commutative law   Ⓐ

B distributive law   Ⓑ

C associative law   Ⓒ

D inverse law   Ⓓ

13 Cubes of side 2 cm are cut off from a large cube of side 8 cm. The number of smaller cubes obtained will be

A 4   Ⓐ

B 16   Ⓑ

C 32   Ⓒ

D 64   Ⓓ

14 An article bought for $160.00 was sold for $200.00. This represents a profit of

A 2.5%   Ⓐ

B 20%   Ⓑ

C 25%   Ⓒ

D 50%   Ⓓ

15 $3(5x - 10y) - 5(-6y + 3x) =$

A $30x - 30y$ Ⓐ

B $-30x + 30y$ Ⓑ

C $45x - 45y$ Ⓒ

D 0   Ⓓ

16 Two sets P and Q are such that $n(P) = 7$, $n(Q) = 5$ and $n(P \cup Q) = 9$. Then $n(P \cap Q) =$

A 2   Ⓐ

B 3   Ⓑ

C 12   Ⓒ

D 21   Ⓓ

17 Given $3.8 \times 0.14 = 0.532$. The value of $380 \times 0.014 =$

A 0.0532   Ⓐ

B 0.532   Ⓑ

C 5.32   Ⓒ

D 53.2   Ⓓ

18 If x is a positive even integer, then $x + 3$ will always be

A odd   Ⓐ

B even   Ⓑ

C prime   Ⓒ

D divisible by 3   Ⓓ

19 $A = \{a, e, i, o, u\}$. The number of subsets of A is

A 5   Ⓐ

B 6   Ⓑ

C 16   Ⓒ

D 32   Ⓓ

20 $\sqrt[3]{\dfrac{-8}{27}}$ is

A $\frac{2}{3}$ Ⓐ

B $-\frac{2}{3}$ Ⓑ

C $\frac{3}{2}$ Ⓒ

D $-\frac{3}{2}$ Ⓓ

21 Jack did $\frac{1}{5}$ of a job and James did $\frac{2}{3}$ of the remainder. The fraction that remains to be done is

A $\frac{4}{15}$ Ⓐ

B $\frac{8}{15}$ Ⓑ

C $\frac{11}{15}$ Ⓒ

D $\frac{4}{5}$ Ⓓ

22 $x^2 - 8x + 7 =$

A $(x+1)(x-7)$ Ⓐ

B $(x-1)(x-7)$ Ⓑ

C $(x-1)(x+7)$ Ⓒ

D $(x+1)(x+7)$ Ⓓ

23 $5x - 2(-2x) + 3x =$

A $-4x$ Ⓐ

B $-6x$ Ⓑ

C $8x$ Ⓒ

D $12x$ Ⓓ

24

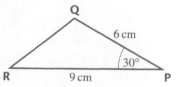

The area of triangle PQR, shown above, is

A $12\,\text{cm}^2$ Ⓐ

B $13.5\,\text{cm}^2$ Ⓑ

C $54\,\text{cm}^2$ Ⓒ

D $60\,\text{cm}^2$ Ⓓ

25 Three men, S, T and R share a sum of money in the ratio of $4:2:3$. The fraction that is T's share is

A $\frac{2}{3}$ Ⓐ

B $\frac{1}{2}$ Ⓑ

C $\frac{2}{9}$ Ⓒ

D $\frac{1}{12}$ Ⓓ

26 In a class each student studies Mathematics or Science or both. 20 students study Mathematics and 20 study Science. If the class has 30 students the number of students who study both subjects is

A   40   Ⓐ

B   30   Ⓑ

C   20   Ⓒ

D   10   Ⓓ

27 A man works for $7.00 an hour and receives $1\frac{1}{2}$ times that for overtime work, in excess of 50 hours per week. His salary for a 60 hour week will be

A $630.00   Ⓐ

B $455.00   Ⓑ

C $350.00   Ⓒ

D $105.00   Ⓓ

28 If $S = \{a, b, c\}$ and $T = (c, d, e, b, f\}$, then

A $S = T$ Ⓐ

B $T \subset S$ Ⓑ

C $S \subset T$ Ⓒ

D $S \cap T \neq \varnothing$ Ⓓ

29

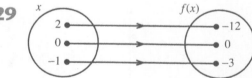

The above mapping can be represented by

A $f(x) = -3x^2$ Ⓐ

B $f(x) = 3x^2$ Ⓑ

C $f(x) = -3x^3$ Ⓒ

D $f(x) = 2x^2$ Ⓓ

30 The transformation matrix $\begin{pmatrix} 1 & 0 \\ 0 & -1 \end{pmatrix}$ represents

A   reflection in the x-axis   Ⓐ

B   reflection in the y-axis   Ⓑ

C   reflection in the line $y = x$ Ⓒ

D   reflection in the line $y = -x$ Ⓓ

31

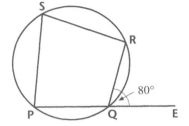

In the figure above (not drawn to scale) PQRS is a quadrilateral inscribed in a circle. PQ is produced to E and ∠RQE = 80°. The size of ∠PSR is

A   110°   Ⓐ
B   100°   Ⓑ
C   90°   Ⓒ
D   80°   Ⓓ

32 The vector $\begin{pmatrix} -4 \\ 3 \end{pmatrix}$ translates a point S (1, 2) onto a point S′. The coordinates of S′ are

A   (5, −1)   Ⓐ
B   (−5, 1)   Ⓑ
C   (−3, 5)   Ⓒ
D   (3, −5)   Ⓓ

33

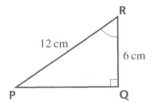

In the figure above, not drawn to scale, the size of ∠PRQ is

A   30°   Ⓐ
B   45°   Ⓑ
C   60°   Ⓒ
D   75°   Ⓓ

34

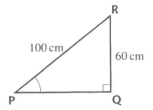

The tangent of ∠QPR is

A $\frac{5}{3}$ Ⓐ
B $\frac{5}{4}$ Ⓑ
C $\frac{3}{4}$ Ⓒ
D $\frac{3}{5}$ Ⓓ

35 A man left a point T at 09:15 hours and drove to a point V, arriving at 15:30 hours. If he had taken a 45 minute lunch break and 10 minutes to refuel his car, the time spent driving was

A   6 hours 15 minutes   Ⓐ
B   5 hours 30 minutes   Ⓑ
C   5 hours 20 minutes   Ⓒ
D   5 hours   Ⓓ

36 The interquartile range of the set of numbers 3, 7, 9, 13, 15, 17, 10, 12 is

A   10   Ⓐ
B   6   Ⓑ
C   5   Ⓒ
D   3   Ⓓ

37 An article marked at $500.00 is increased by 10% just before a sale and then given a 10% discount at the sale. The sale price of the item is

A $500.00   Ⓐ
B $495.00   Ⓑ
C $490.00   Ⓒ
D $480.00   Ⓓ

38 A man sold a bicycle for $360.00, losing 20% on what he had paid. The price paid was

A $380.00 Ⓐ
B $400.00 Ⓑ
C $432.00 Ⓒ
D $450.00 Ⓓ

39

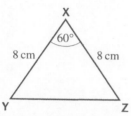

In the figure above, not drawn to scale, the triangle XYZ is isosceles with XY = XZ = 8 cm. The area of triangle XYZ is

A $16\sqrt{3}\,\text{cm}^2$ Ⓐ
B $32\sqrt{3}\,\text{cm}^2$ Ⓑ
C $36\sqrt{3}\,\text{cm}^2$ Ⓒ
D $46\,\text{cm}^2$ Ⓓ

40 $(2a^2b)^3 \div (2a^3b)^2 =$

A 1 Ⓐ
B $8ab$ Ⓑ
C $2a^2b$ Ⓒ
D $2b$ Ⓓ

41 The sum of the exterior angles of a regular hexagon is

A 120° Ⓐ
B 180° Ⓑ
C 360° Ⓒ
D 720° Ⓓ

42

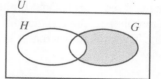

The Universal set represents the students in a class.
H = {students who study History}
G = {students who study Geography}
The shaded region represents

A all students in the class who do not study History Ⓐ
B all students who study Geography Ⓑ
C all students who study Geography but not History Ⓒ
D students who study both History and Geography only Ⓓ

43 From 03:15 hours to 05:15 hours, the hour hand of a clock rotates through an angle of

A 60° Ⓐ
B 90° Ⓑ
C 270° Ⓒ
D 720° Ⓓ

44

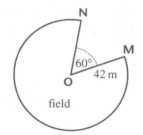

A field is shaped like a major sector of a circle of radius 42 m (as shown in the diagram). An athlete starts from O and runs from O to M, along the arc MN and then from N to O. The distance covered is

A 308 m Ⓐ
B 304 m Ⓑ
C 264 m Ⓒ
D 220 m Ⓓ

45 A bag contains 8 red marbles and 6 blue marbles. A marble is picked at random from the bag. The probability that it is not blue is

A $\frac{1}{7}$ Ⓐ

B $\frac{3}{7}$ Ⓑ

C $\frac{4}{7}$ Ⓒ

D $\frac{3}{4}$ Ⓓ

46 The mean of a set of 8 numbers is 3.5. If the number 8 is added to the set, then the new mean is

A 8.0   Ⓐ

B 4.5   Ⓑ

C 4.0   Ⓒ

D 3.5   Ⓓ

47

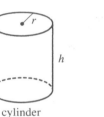
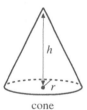

cylinder   cone

The ratio of the volume of the cylinder to the volume of the cone is

A $3^3 : 1^3$ Ⓐ

B $1^2 : 3^2$ Ⓑ

C $1 : 3$ Ⓒ

D $3 : 1$ Ⓓ

Questions 48–50 refer to the table below which shows the scores obtained by 30 students in a quiz.

Score	0	1	2	3	4	5
Number of students	1	4	6	6	9	4

48 The modal score is

A 2   Ⓐ

B 4   Ⓑ

C 6   Ⓒ

D 9   Ⓓ

49 The mean score is

A 2   Ⓐ

B 3   Ⓑ

C 4   Ⓒ

D 5   Ⓓ

50 The probability that a student chosen at random scored either 2 or 3 correct answers is

A $\frac{1}{6}$ Ⓐ

B $\frac{1}{5}$ Ⓑ

C $\frac{2}{5}$ Ⓒ

D $\frac{1}{2}$ Ⓓ

51

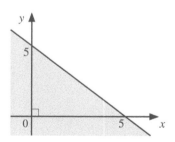

The shaded region shows the set of points (x, y) such that

A $x + y \leq 5$ Ⓐ

B $x - y \leq 5$ Ⓑ

C $x - y \geq 5$ Ⓒ

D $-x - y \geq 5$ Ⓓ

52 A certain number, x, is trebled and then cubed. The result is

A $3x^3$ Ⓐ
B $6x^3$ Ⓑ
C $9x^3$ Ⓒ
D $27x^3$ Ⓓ

53 A has twice as many marbles as B who has twice as many as C. If the total number of marbles is 84, then B has

A 12 marbles   Ⓐ
B 24 marbles   Ⓑ
C 36 marbles   Ⓒ
D 48 marbles   Ⓓ

54 A cube has the same volume as a cuboid of length 8 cm, width 9 cm and height 3 cm. The length of a side of the cube is

A 36 cm   Ⓐ
B 27 cm   Ⓑ
C 12 cm   Ⓒ
D   6 cm   Ⓓ

Numbers 55–57 refer to the graph below.

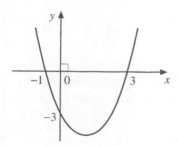

55 The equation representing the graph above is

A $y = -x^2 - 2x + 3$ Ⓐ
B $y = x^2 - 2x - 3$ Ⓑ
C $y = x^2 + 2x - 3$ Ⓒ
D $y = x^2 + 2x + 3$ Ⓓ

56 The set of values of x for which $y > 0$ is

A $x < 3$ and $x > -3$ Ⓐ
B $x < 3$ and $x > 1$ Ⓑ
C $x < -1$ or $x > 3$ Ⓒ
D $x > -3$ or $x < -1$ Ⓓ

57 The axis of symmetry of the graph is

A $x = -3$ Ⓐ
B $x = -1$ Ⓑ
C $x = 1$ Ⓒ
D $x = 3$ Ⓓ

58 $(a - b)^2 - (x - y)^2 =$

A $(a - b + x - y)(a - b - x - y)$ Ⓐ
B $(a + b + x + y)(a - b - x - y)$ Ⓑ
C $(a - b + x - y)(a + b - x + y)$ Ⓒ
D $(a - b - x + y)(a - b + x - y)$ Ⓓ

59

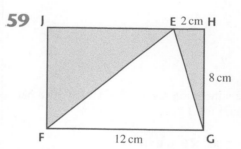

E is a point on the side JH of a rectangle FGHJ. FG = 12 cm, GH = 8 cm and EH = 2 cm. The total shaded area is

A $16 \, cm^2$ Ⓐ
B $48 \, cm^2$ Ⓑ
C $80 \, cm^2$ Ⓒ
D $96 \, cm^2$ Ⓓ

60 If $2(3x - 1) > 2x - 10$, then

A $x > 2$ Ⓐ
B $x < 2$ Ⓑ
C $x > -2$ Ⓒ
D $x < -2$ Ⓓ

Test number 5

Read the directions on page (iv) carefully.

1   25.13 in standard form is

    A 2.513×10^{-3} Ⓐ

    B 2.513×10^{-2} Ⓑ

    C 2.513×10^{-1} Ⓒ

    D 2.513×10^{1} Ⓓ

2   0.65 may be written as

    A $\frac{1}{2}$ Ⓐ

    B $\frac{11}{20}$ Ⓑ

    C $\frac{3}{5}$ Ⓒ

    D $\frac{13}{20}$ Ⓓ

3   The simple interest on \$600.00 at 10% per annum for 3 years is

    A $\$\dfrac{600 \times 3 \times 100}{10}$ Ⓐ

    B $\$\dfrac{600 \times 3 \times 10}{100}$ Ⓑ

    C $\$\dfrac{600 \times 100 \times 10}{3}$ Ⓒ

    D $\$\dfrac{600 \times 3}{100}$ Ⓓ

4   The median of the set of numbers 7, 3, 11, 1, 2, 5, 6, 6, 2 is

    A   2   Ⓐ

    B   3   Ⓑ

    C   5   Ⓒ

    D   11   Ⓓ

5 $y^{\frac{1}{4}}$ means

    A   the 4th root of y Ⓐ

    B $\frac{1}{4}$ of y Ⓑ

    C   4 times y Ⓒ

    D $y \times y \times y \times y$ Ⓓ

6

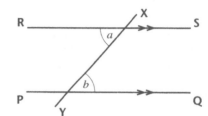

   PQ and RS are 2 parallel lines cut by a transversal XY, as shown in the diagram above. The relation between a and b is

    A $a > b$ Ⓐ

    B $a < b$ Ⓑ

    C $a \neq b$ Ⓒ

    D $a = b$ Ⓓ

7   An item now worth \$7200.00 was originally bought for \$8000.00. Its depreciation is

    A   20%   Ⓐ

    B   18%   Ⓑ

    C   10%   Ⓒ

    D   5%   Ⓓ

8

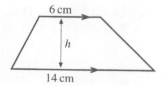

The figure above illustrates a trapezium of area $40\,cm^2$. Its height, h, is

A $4\,cm$

B $8\,cm$

C $10\,cm$

D $12\,cm$

9

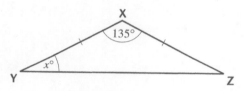

In the figure above, XYZ is a triangle with $XY = XZ$ and $\angle YXZ = 135°$. The size of x is

A $22\frac{1}{2}°$

B $45°$

C $67\frac{1}{2}°$

D $70°$

10 A fair coin was tossed twice. The probability of obtaining 2 heads in the 2 tosses is

A 1

B $\frac{3}{4}$

C $\frac{1}{2}$

D $\frac{1}{4}$

11 The mean of the set of numbers 3, 6, 8, 13, 15 is

A 8

B 9

C 10

D 12

12 The set of prime factors of 6 is

A $\{1, 2, 3, 6\}$

B $\{1, 2, 3\}$

C $\{2, 3\}$

D $\{1, 3\}$

13 If $\dfrac{3}{x} - 3 = 3$, then $x =$

A 9

B 6

C 3

D $\frac{1}{2}$

14 Which of the following mappings illustrate a function?

(i)

(ii)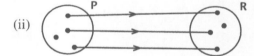

(iii)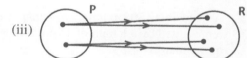

(iv)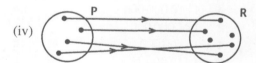

A (i) and (ii) only

B (i), (ii) and (iii) only

C (i) and (iv) only

D (ii) and (iv) only

15 A man works for $7.00 per hour up to 40 hours a week. He gets paid $1\frac{1}{2}$ times this rate for overtime. What will his week's pay amount to if he works 10 hours overtime?

A $105.00

B $200.00

C $315.00

D $385.00

16 The size of each interior angle of a regular octagon is

A   180°   Ⓐ
B   135°   Ⓑ
C   108°   Ⓒ
D   90°   Ⓓ

17 The compound interest on $10 000.00 at 5% compounded yearly for 2 years is

A $1100.00   Ⓐ
B $1025.00   Ⓑ
C $1000.00   Ⓒ
D $875.00   Ⓓ

18 In a regular polygon of n sides, each exterior angle is 72°. The value of n is

A   8   Ⓐ
B   7   Ⓑ
C   6   Ⓒ
D   5   Ⓓ

19 An island is 150 km long. On a map it is represented by a length of 15 cm. The scale of the map is

A   1 : 10 000 000 Ⓐ
B   1 : 1 000 000   Ⓑ
C   1 : 100 000   Ⓒ
D   1 : 10 000   Ⓓ

20 38.47 to 3 significant figures is

A   38.0   Ⓐ
B   38.5   Ⓑ
C   39.0   Ⓒ
D   40.0   Ⓓ

21 In 2103_5, the value of 1 is

A 1×5^0 Ⓐ
B 1×5^1 Ⓑ
C 1×5^2 Ⓒ
D 1×5^3 Ⓓ

22 Given that y is proportional to x. This relationship can be illustrated graphically by

A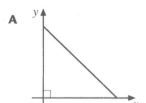

B   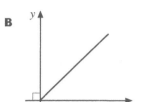   Ⓑ

C   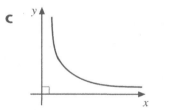   Ⓒ

D   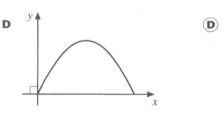   Ⓓ

23 If $P = \{$factors of 8$\}$ and $Q = \{$factors of 12$\}$, then $n(P \cap Q) =$

A   2   Ⓐ
B   3   Ⓑ
C   4   Ⓒ
D   6   Ⓓ

24 If $g(x) = \dfrac{3 - x}{x}$, $x \neq 0$, then $g(-1) =$

A   −4   Ⓐ
B   −2   Ⓑ
C   2   Ⓒ
D   4   Ⓓ

25

The figure shows a solid, right, circular cylinder of base radius r and height h. Its total surface area is given by

A $\pi r^2 h$ Ⓐ
B $2\pi rh$ Ⓑ
C $2\pi rh + \pi r^2$ Ⓒ
D $2\pi rh + 2\pi r^2$ Ⓓ

26

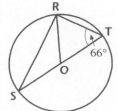

The figure above, not drawn to scale, shows a circle, centre O. ST is a diameter and R is a point on the circumference such that angle OTR = 66°. The size of the angle RST is

A   24°   Ⓐ
B   32°   Ⓑ
C   33°   Ⓒ
D   48°   Ⓓ

27

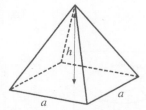

The figure shows a pyramid with a square base, and side a and height h. The volume is

A $\frac{1}{4}a^2h^2$ Ⓐ
B $\frac{1}{2}a^2h$ Ⓑ
C $\frac{1}{3}a^2h$ Ⓒ
D $\frac{1}{3}ah^2$ Ⓓ

28 Out of 175 students who wrote an examination, 55 were successful. The probability that a randomly chosen student was unsuccessful is

A $\frac{11}{20}$ Ⓐ
B $\frac{11}{24}$ Ⓑ
C $\frac{3}{4}$ Ⓒ
D $\frac{24}{35}$ Ⓓ

29 $\sqrt{\dfrac{1.44}{100}}$ is

A   1.2   Ⓐ
B   0.12   Ⓑ
C   0.012   Ⓒ
D   0.0144   Ⓓ

30 1 hectometre is what percentage of a kilometre?

A   1000%   Ⓐ
B   100%   Ⓑ
C   10%   Ⓒ
D   1%   Ⓓ

31 PQ is the diameter of the circle, centre O. R is a point on the circumference such that PR = 8 cm and QR = 6 cm. The radius of the circle is

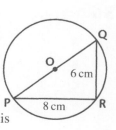

A   5 cm   Ⓐ
B   7 cm   Ⓑ
C   10 cm   Ⓒ
D   14 cm   Ⓓ

32 An item was bought for $210.00 and sold for $280.00. The percentage profit was

A   25%   Ⓐ
B $33\frac{1}{3}$%   Ⓑ
C   70%   Ⓒ
D   75%   Ⓓ

33 The mean of 8 numbers is 31. The number 22 is added. The new mean is

A   34.2   Ⓐ
B   33.75   Ⓑ
C   31   Ⓒ
D   30   Ⓓ

34 The number x is cubed and diminished by 2. If the result is trebled, then this may be expressed algebraically as

A $3(x^3 - 2)$ Ⓐ
B $3(2 - x^3)$ Ⓑ
C $\dfrac{\sqrt[3]{x} + 2}{3}$ Ⓒ
D $3(\sqrt[3]{x} - 2)$ Ⓓ

35 $e^2 - 9 =$

A $-(e - 3)(e - 3)$ Ⓐ
B $(e + 3)(e + 3)$ Ⓑ
C $(e - 3)(e - 3)$ Ⓒ
D $(e - 3)(e + 3)$ Ⓓ

36 $(-2)^{-3} =$

A $-\dfrac{1}{8}$ Ⓐ
B $\dfrac{1}{8}$ Ⓑ
C -8 Ⓒ
D 8 Ⓓ

37 Given that $1.00 \text{ US} \equiv \$6.42 \text{ TT}$. The amount in US dollars that is equivalent to $256.80 TT is

A $36.72 US   Ⓐ
B $38.14 US   Ⓑ
C $40.00 US   Ⓒ
D $42.50 US   Ⓓ

38 A man buys a washing machine with a downpayment of $120.00 and payments of $45.00 per month for 2 years. How much would he have saved by buying it cash for $950.00?

A $200.00   Ⓐ
B $250.00   Ⓑ
C $265.00   Ⓒ
D $315.00   Ⓓ

39 $a(2b + c) - a(2b - c) =$

A $4ab + 2ac$ Ⓐ
B $4ab - 2ac$ Ⓑ
C $4ab$ Ⓒ
D $2ac$ Ⓓ

40 A table on sale was given a 15% discount. The table was sold for $680.00. Its original price was

A $800.00   Ⓐ
B $790.00   Ⓑ
C $782.00   Ⓒ
D $695.00   Ⓓ

41 Given that V is inversely proportional to T and that V is 8 when T is 4. The value of V when T is 12 is

A   24   Ⓐ
B   2   Ⓑ
C $2\dfrac{2}{3}$ Ⓒ
D $\dfrac{3}{8}$ Ⓓ

42

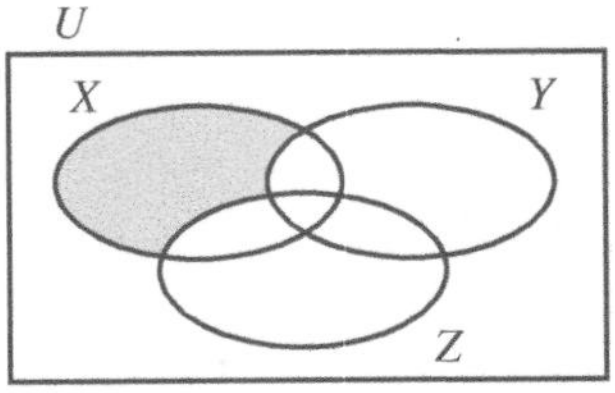

In the Venn diagram above, the shaded region represents

A $(Y \cup Z)' \cap X$ Ⓐ
B $(Y \cup Z) \cap X$ Ⓑ
C $X \cap Y'$ Ⓒ
D $Y \cap X'$ Ⓓ

43 If M = {factors of 6}, N = {factors of 4}, P = {factors of 5}, $n(M \cap N \cap P)$ =

A 1 Ⓐ
B 2 Ⓑ
C 3 Ⓒ
D 4 Ⓓ

44 26_{10} written in base 2 is

A 11010_2 Ⓐ
B 10101_2 Ⓑ
C 10001_2 Ⓒ
D 10011_2 Ⓓ

45

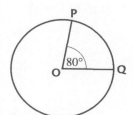

The diagram shows a circle, centre O, of area 9 cm^2. If $\angle POQ = 80°$, then the area of the major sector POQ is

A 2 cm^2 Ⓐ
B 5 cm^2 Ⓑ
C 7 cm^2 Ⓒ
D 11 cm^2 Ⓓ

46 If $p = 2$, $q = -1$, $r = 3$ then $(pq)^r$ =

A 8 Ⓐ
B 6 Ⓑ
C -6 Ⓒ
D -8 Ⓓ

47 If $v = u + at$, then a =

A $\dfrac{v + u}{t}$ Ⓐ

B $\dfrac{v - u}{t}$ Ⓑ

C $(v - u) \times t$ Ⓒ
D $(v + t) \div u$ Ⓓ

48 A man drove from a point P to a point Q, leaving P at 09:20 hrs and arriving at Q at 14:40 hrs. If the distance between P and Q is 300 km and he stopped for a 20 minute lunch break, his average speed was

A $56\frac{1}{4} \text{ km h}^{-1}$ Ⓐ
B 60 km h^{-1} Ⓑ
C $64\frac{1}{2} \text{ km h}^{-1}$ Ⓒ
D 65 km h^{-1} Ⓓ

49 If $a * b$ denotes $2a^b$ then $2 * 3$ =

A 12 Ⓐ
B 16 Ⓑ
C 32 Ⓒ
D 64 Ⓓ

50 Q = {quadrilaterals}, P = {parallelograms} and R = {rectangles}. The Venn diagram which illustrates this is

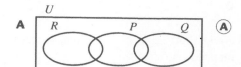

A Ⓐ

B Ⓑ

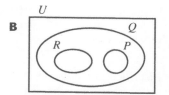

C Ⓒ

D Ⓓ

51 A sum of money is divided among A, B and C in the ratio $2 : 5 : 4$ respectively. If C receives $10.00 less than B, then the total sum shared is

A $40.00   Ⓐ
B $90.00   Ⓑ
C $110.00   Ⓒ
D $120.00   Ⓓ

52

In the right-angled triangle above, the cosine of the angle G is

A $\dfrac{a}{c}$ Ⓐ

B $\dfrac{c}{a}$ Ⓑ

C $\dfrac{c}{b}$ Ⓒ

D $\dfrac{b}{c}$ Ⓓ

53 Given that $f : x \to 2x^2$, an element that is mapped onto itself is

A -1 Ⓐ
B 1 Ⓑ
C 0 Ⓒ
D 2 Ⓓ

54 A sphere is inscribed in a cube so that it touches the six faces of the cube. If the cube is of side 4 cm, the volume of the sphere is

A $32\pi \, \text{cm}^3$ Ⓐ

B $16\frac{2}{3}\pi \, \text{cm}^3$ Ⓑ

C $10\frac{2}{3}\pi \, \text{cm}^3$ Ⓒ

D $6\pi \, \text{cm}^3$ Ⓓ

55 $\sqrt{300}$ to three significant figures is approximately

A 1.73×10^2 Ⓐ
B 1.73×10 Ⓑ
C 1.73×10^{-1} Ⓒ
D 1.73×10^{-2} Ⓓ

Questions 56–58 refer to the diagram below.

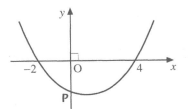

56 The equation of the quadratic graph is

A $y = x^2 + 2x + 8$ Ⓐ
B $y = -x^2 - 2x + 8$ Ⓑ
C $y = x^2 + 2x - 8$ Ⓒ
D $y = x^2 - 2x - 8$ Ⓓ

57 The coordinates of the point P are

A $(-8, 0)$ Ⓐ
B $(-4, 0)$ Ⓑ
C $(0, -8)$ Ⓒ
D $(0, -4)$ Ⓓ

58 The range of values of x for which y is less than zero is

A $-2 \le x < 4$ Ⓐ
B $-2 < x < 4$ Ⓑ
C $-2 < x \le 4$ Ⓒ
D $-2 \le x \le 4$ Ⓓ

59 The number $312_n \equiv 54_{10}$. The value of n is

A   4   Ⓐ
B   5   Ⓑ
C   6   Ⓒ
D   7   Ⓓ

60 The following table shows the marks out of 5 obtained by students in a science test.

Marks	0	1	2	3	4	5
Number of students	4	2	3	7	2	2

The mean mark is

A   0.75   Ⓐ
B   1.00   Ⓑ
C   2.35   Ⓒ
D   3.00   Ⓓ

Test number ⑥

Read the directions on page (iv) carefully.

1

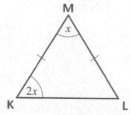

In the figure above, the size of angle KLM is

A   36°   Ⓐ
B   72°   Ⓑ
C   108°   Ⓒ
D   144°   Ⓓ

2   An item marked at \$60.00 is given a 20% discount at a sale. The sale price of the item is

A   \$48.00   Ⓐ
B   \$40.00   Ⓑ
C   \$24.00   Ⓒ
D   \$12.00   Ⓓ

3   0.075 written as a common fraction is

A $\frac{3}{4}$ Ⓐ
B $\frac{3}{40}$ Ⓑ
C $\frac{3}{400}$ Ⓒ
D $\frac{3}{4000}$ Ⓓ

4 $3x - 3(2 + x) =$

A $6x - 6$ Ⓐ
B $-6x - 6$ Ⓑ
C $-6x + 6$ Ⓒ
D -6 Ⓓ

5   The value of $(-2a)(3a)(-a)$ is

A $6a^3$ Ⓐ
B $6a$ Ⓑ
C $-6a^3$ Ⓒ
D $-6a$ Ⓓ

6   An even number n is added to 3; the resulting number will always be

A   odd   Ⓐ
B   even   Ⓑ
C   prime   Ⓒ
D   negative   Ⓓ

7   The number 0.0158 written to 3 significant figures is

A   0.02   Ⓐ
B   0.016   Ⓑ
C   0.0158   Ⓒ
D   0.015   Ⓓ

8   The set of integers $\{x: 2 < x \le 6\}$ can be listed as

A   {2, 3, 4, 5, 6}   Ⓐ
B   {3, 4, 5, 6}   Ⓑ
C   {3, 4, 5}   Ⓒ
D   {2, 4, 6}   Ⓓ

9   The simple interest earned on \$17 000.00 for four years at 5% per annum is

A   \$340.00   Ⓐ
B   \$1 360.00   Ⓑ
C   \$3 400.00   Ⓒ
D   \$13 600.00   Ⓓ

10 $3(2x - 3y) - 2(2x - 2y) =$

  A $2x - 13y$ Ⓐ
  B $12x - 9y$ Ⓑ
  C $10x - 5y$ Ⓒ
  D $2x - 5y$ Ⓓ

11 The set of factors of 9 is

  A $\{3, 9\}$ Ⓐ
  B $\{1, 3, 9\}$ Ⓑ
  C $\{1, 2, 3, 4, 5, 6, 7, 8, 9\}$ Ⓒ
  D $\{9, 18, 27, 36, \ldots\}$ Ⓓ

12 Which of the following diagrams represents a function?

  A 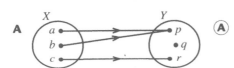   Ⓐ

  B 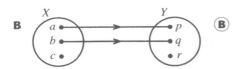   Ⓑ

  C 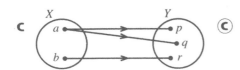   Ⓒ

  D 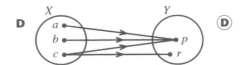   Ⓓ

13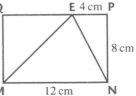

In the figure above MNPQ is a rectangle with MN = 12 cm, NP = 8 cm. The point E on PQ is such that EP = 4 cm. The ratio of the area of triangle MNE to the area of triangle NPE is

  A $3 : 1$ Ⓐ
  B $2 : 1$ Ⓑ
  C $1 : 2$ Ⓒ
  D $1 : 3$ Ⓓ

14 The square of x is divided by the cube of y. The result is

  A $\dfrac{x^2}{\sqrt[3]{y}}$ Ⓐ

  B $\dfrac{x^2}{y^3}$ Ⓑ

  C $\dfrac{\sqrt{x}}{y^3}$ Ⓒ

  D $\dfrac{\sqrt{x}}{\sqrt[3]{y}}$ Ⓓ

15 A washing machine can be bought with a down payment of $120.00 and 12 monthly instalments of $240.00. Alternatively the washing machine may be bought with no down payment and 12 monthly instalments of $250.00. The difference between the two plans is

  A $240.00   Ⓐ
  B $180.00   Ⓑ
  C $120.00   Ⓒ
  D $0.00   Ⓓ

16 $1\frac{4}{9} \div 3\frac{1}{4} =$

  A $\dfrac{169}{36}$ Ⓐ

  B $\dfrac{26}{13}$ Ⓑ

  C $\dfrac{4}{9}$ Ⓒ

  D $\dfrac{1}{9}$ Ⓓ

17 Jack and John share a sum of money in the ratio 2 : 3. The difference in their shares is $60.00. The total amount shared is

A $360.00   Ⓐ
B $300.00   Ⓑ
C $100.00   Ⓒ
D $120.00   Ⓓ

18 The point (3, 4) under reflection in the x-axis is

A (3, −4)   Ⓐ
B (−3, −4)   Ⓑ
C (−4, 3)   Ⓒ
D (−4, −3)   Ⓓ

19 $0.01 \div 0.001 =$

A 0.000 01   Ⓐ
B 0.01   Ⓑ
C 10   Ⓒ
D 100   Ⓓ

20 If $300.00 earned $36.00 simple interest in 2 years, the rate per annum was

A 6%   Ⓐ
B 5%   Ⓑ
C 4%   Ⓒ
D 3%   Ⓓ

21 The transformation matrix $\begin{pmatrix} 0 & 1 \\ 1 & 0 \end{pmatrix}$ represents a

A reflection in the x-axis   Ⓐ
B reflection in the y-axis   Ⓑ
C reflection in the line $y = x$ Ⓒ
D rotation of 90° about O   Ⓓ

22 A boy receives 3 times as much allowance as his sister. Together they receive $28.00 per week. The boy's weekly allowance is

A $7.00   Ⓐ
B $14.00   Ⓑ
C $21.00   Ⓒ
D $28.00   Ⓓ

23 A cuboid of base 6 cm by 8 cm has the same volume as a cube of side 12 cm. The height of the cuboid is

A 12 cm   Ⓐ
B 24 cm   Ⓑ
C 36 cm   Ⓒ
D 48 cm   Ⓓ

24 Workers at a factory receive $10.50 per hour and trainees $\frac{2}{3}$ of this rate. If there are 22 workers and 8 trainees, the total daily wages of the workers and trainees for an 8 hour day will be

A $2520.00   Ⓐ
B $2296.00   Ⓑ
C $1680.00   Ⓒ
D $1050.00   Ⓓ

25 $(3a^2)^{-3} =$

A $\dfrac{a^{-5}}{27}$ Ⓐ

B $\dfrac{a^{-6}}{27}$ Ⓑ

C $9a^{-6}$ Ⓒ

D $3a^{-8}$ Ⓓ

26 The sides of 2 triangles are 6 cm, 8 cm, 10 cm and 5 cm, 12 cm and 13 cm respectively. The two triangles are

A similar   Ⓐ
B right-angled   Ⓑ
C congruent   Ⓒ
D isosceles   Ⓓ

27 If $f(x) = 3x^4$ then $f(x^2) =$

A $3x^4$ Ⓐ
B $3x^8$ Ⓑ
C $9x^8$ Ⓒ
D $9x^{16}$ Ⓓ

28 If A = {multiples of 2, less than 10}
and B = {multiples of 3, less than 10},
then $n(A \cap B)$

A   0   Ⓐ
B   1   Ⓑ
C   4   Ⓒ
D   6   Ⓓ

29

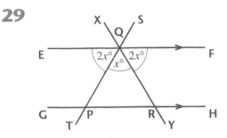

EF and GH are two parallel lines. ST cuts
EF at Q and GH at P. XY cuts EF at Q and
GH at R. $\angle EQP = \angle FQR = 2x°$ and
$\angle PQR = x°$. $\angle QRP =$

A   36°   Ⓐ
B   54°   Ⓑ
C   72°   Ⓒ
D   80°   Ⓓ

30

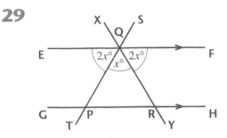

The area of trapezium QRST is

A   60 cm^2 Ⓐ
B   56 cm^2 Ⓑ
C   44 cm^2 Ⓒ
D   32 cm^2 Ⓓ

31

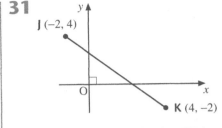

The gradient of the line JK is

A -1 Ⓐ
B $-\frac{1}{2}$ Ⓑ
C $\frac{1}{2}$ Ⓒ
D   1   Ⓓ

32 Between 12:00 noon and 1:00 pm, the hour
hand of a clock rotates through an angle of

A   360°   Ⓐ
B   180°   Ⓑ
C   90°   Ⓒ
D   30°   Ⓓ

*Questions 33–35 refer to the table below. A
survey was conducted on the number of children
in families. The results are shown in the table.*

Number of children	0	1	2	3	4	5	6
Number of families	5	8	11	12	6	2	1

33 The number of families surveyed was

A   12   Ⓐ
B   21   Ⓑ
C   40   Ⓒ
D   45   Ⓓ

34 The modal number of children per family is

A   45   Ⓐ
B   12   Ⓑ
C   11   Ⓒ
D   3   Ⓓ

35 The probability that a family chosen at random has at least 4 children is

A $\frac{1}{15}$ Ⓐ

B $\frac{2}{15}$ Ⓑ

C $\frac{1}{5}$ Ⓒ

D $\frac{14}{15}$ Ⓓ

36 The number of axes of symmetry in a square is

A 2   Ⓐ

B 3   Ⓑ

C 4   Ⓒ

D 6   Ⓓ

37 If $2\begin{pmatrix} 2 & 3 \\ -1 & a \end{pmatrix} = \begin{pmatrix} 4 & 6 \\ -2 & 6 \end{pmatrix}$, then $a =$

A 6   Ⓐ

B 4   Ⓑ

C 3   Ⓒ

E 2   Ⓓ

38 On a certain day the probability that a man wears a red tie is $\frac{2}{7}$ and the probability that he wears a blue suit is $\frac{1}{2}$. The probability that the man does not wear a red tie and wears a blue suit is

A $\frac{1}{7}$ Ⓐ

B $\frac{9}{14}$ Ⓑ

C $\frac{1}{2}$ Ⓒ

D $\frac{5}{14}$ Ⓓ

39 A plane is travelling on a bearing of 224°. This direction lies between

A south and west   Ⓐ

B north and west   Ⓑ

C north and east   Ⓒ

D south and east   Ⓓ

40 The diagram shows a chord AB drawn on a circle, centre O. D is a point on the circumference and ∠OAB = 30°. The size of ∠ADB is

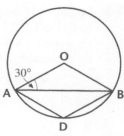

A 90°   Ⓐ

B 120°   Ⓑ

C 140°   Ⓒ

D 180°   Ⓓ

41 The radius of a circular lake is 77 m. The circumference of the lake is

A 484 m   Ⓐ

B 400 m   Ⓑ

C 318 m   Ⓒ

D 242 m   Ⓓ

42 If $f(x) = 2x^2$ and $g(x) = x + 2$, then $gf(2) =$

A 10   Ⓐ

B 16   Ⓑ

C 32   Ⓒ

D 40   Ⓓ

43

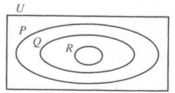

The Venn diagram illustrates three sets P, Q, R. The following statements have been made:

I $R \subset Q$

II $P \cap Q = P$

III $P \cup Q \cup R = P$

IV $P \supset Q$

The true statements are

A II and III only   Ⓐ

B I, III and IV only   Ⓑ

C I, II and III only   Ⓒ

D all four statements   Ⓓ

44 In a class of 20 students, 8 students like basketball and 7 students like football. If no student likes both games, the probability that a student chosen at random likes neither game is

A $\frac{3}{4}$ Ⓐ

B $\frac{2}{5}$ Ⓑ

C $\frac{7}{20}$ Ⓒ

D $\frac{1}{4}$ Ⓓ

45

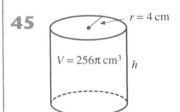

The figure shows a right circular cylinder of radius, $r = 4\,cm$. If the volume of the cylinder is $256\pi\,cm^3$, the height is

A   8 cm   Ⓐ
B   12 cm   Ⓑ
C   16 cm   Ⓒ
D   24 cm   Ⓓ

46

The line graph represents

A $x \le 2$ or $x > 6$ Ⓐ
B $x < 2$ or $x \ge 6$ Ⓑ
C $x < 2$ Ⓒ
D $x \ge 6$ Ⓓ

47 Given that y varies as the square of x and inversely as the square root of z. Then

A $y \propto \dfrac{z^2}{\sqrt{x}}$ Ⓐ

B $y \propto \dfrac{\sqrt{z}}{x^2}$ Ⓑ

C $y \propto \dfrac{\sqrt{x}}{z^2}$ Ⓒ

D $y \propto \dfrac{x^2}{\sqrt{z}}$ Ⓓ

48 An article bought for $84.00 is to be sold at a profit of 25%. The selling price should be

A $67.20   Ⓐ
B $90.80   Ⓑ
C $105.00   Ⓒ
D $125.00   Ⓓ

49 If $a = \begin{pmatrix} 4 \\ 1 \end{pmatrix}$ and $b = \begin{pmatrix} -2 \\ -8 \end{pmatrix}$, then the resultant of a and b is

A $\begin{pmatrix} -2 \\ 7 \end{pmatrix}$ Ⓐ

B $\begin{pmatrix} -6 \\ -9 \end{pmatrix}$ Ⓑ

C $\begin{pmatrix} 6 \\ 9 \end{pmatrix}$ Ⓒ

D $\begin{pmatrix} 2 \\ -7 \end{pmatrix}$ Ⓓ

50 A plane leaves V at 14:00 hrs and arrives at W at 17:30 hrs. The distance between V and W is 1925 km. The average speed of travel is

A $550\,km\,h^{-1}$ Ⓐ
B $600\,km\,h^{-1}$ Ⓑ
C $625\,km\,h^{-1}$ Ⓒ
D $650\,km\,h^{-1}$ Ⓓ

51 If $X = \begin{bmatrix} 2 & 3 \\ 4 & -1 \end{bmatrix}$ then the determinant of X is

A -10 Ⓐ
B -14 Ⓑ
C 10 Ⓒ
D 14 Ⓓ

52 If $X = \begin{pmatrix} 1 & 2 \\ -2 & 3 \end{pmatrix}$ and $Y = \begin{pmatrix} -1 & -2 \\ 2 & -3 \end{pmatrix}$ then $X - 2Y =$

A $\begin{pmatrix} 3 & 6 \\ -6 & 9 \end{pmatrix}$ Ⓐ

B $\begin{pmatrix} 0 & 0 \\ 0 & 0 \end{pmatrix}$ Ⓑ

C $\begin{pmatrix} 3 & -6 \\ 6 & -9 \end{pmatrix}$ Ⓒ

D $\begin{pmatrix} -3 & -6 \\ 6 & 9 \end{pmatrix}$ Ⓓ

53 In a garden, a farmer uses 30% of his land for planting vegetables. This could be represented on a pie chart by a sector of angle

A 30° Ⓐ
B 90° Ⓑ
C 108° Ⓒ
D 120° Ⓓ

54 In the number 3142_5, the digit 1 has a value, written in base 10, of

A 1 Ⓐ
B 5 Ⓑ
C 25 Ⓒ
D 100 Ⓓ

55

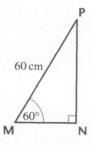

In the triangle MNP, $\angle PMN = 60°$ and $\angle PNM = 90°$. If MP = 60 cm then MN =

A 90 cm Ⓐ
B 60 cm Ⓑ
C 45 cm Ⓒ
D 30 cm Ⓓ

56 If $a = 1$, and $b = -1$, then $(a - b)^3 =$

A 8 Ⓐ
B 6 Ⓑ
C 0 Ⓒ
D −6 Ⓓ

57 If $\cos \angle A = -\frac{3}{5}$ and $\angle A$ is obtuse, then $\sin \angle A =$

A $-\frac{4}{5}$ Ⓐ
B $-\frac{3}{5}$ Ⓑ
C $\frac{3}{5}$ Ⓒ
D $\frac{4}{5}$ Ⓓ

58 $x^2 - (b + c)^2 =$

A $(x + b - c)(x - b + c)$ Ⓐ
B $(x - b - c)(x - b - c)$ Ⓑ
C $(x - b - c)(x + b + c)$ Ⓒ
D $(x - b + c)(x - b - c)$ Ⓓ

59 24_{10} written in binary form is

A 11 000 Ⓐ
B 10 101 Ⓑ
C 10 001 Ⓒ
D 11 010 Ⓓ

60

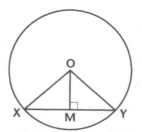

In the above diagram XY is a chord of the circle, centre O. OM is perpendicular to XY. If OM = 6 cm and XY = 16 cm then the diameter of the circle is

A 10 cm Ⓐ
B 14 cm Ⓑ
C 20 cm Ⓒ
D 24 cm Ⓓ

Test number 7

Read the directions on page (iv) carefully.

1 $3a^{-2} \times -2a^3 =$

  A $6a^{-5}$ Ⓐ

  B $6a^{-6}$ Ⓑ

  C $-6a$ Ⓒ

  D $-6a^5$ Ⓓ

2 0.375 as a fraction in its lowest terms is

  A $\frac{3}{8}$ Ⓐ

  B $\frac{4}{8}$ Ⓑ

  C $\frac{5}{8}$ Ⓒ

  D $\frac{7}{8}$ Ⓓ

3 If 30% of a number is 30, the number is

  A 1   Ⓐ

  B 60   Ⓑ

  C 90   Ⓒ

  D 100   Ⓓ

4 $2.2 \div 0.02 =$

  A 110   Ⓐ

  B 11.0   Ⓑ

  C 1.10   Ⓒ

  D 0.11   Ⓓ

5 A sum of money is divided among 3 men P, Q and R in the ratio of $2 : 3 : 5$ respectively. The difference between P and R's share as a fraction of the total is

  A $\frac{5}{8}$ Ⓐ

  B $\frac{3}{10}$ Ⓑ

  C $\frac{1}{5}$ Ⓒ

  D $\frac{1}{10}$ Ⓓ

6 If $S = \{x : 5 \leq x \leq 15; x \in Z\}$ then $n(S) =$

  A 3   Ⓐ

  B 6   Ⓑ

  C 10   Ⓒ

  D 11   Ⓓ

7 A truck left a town V at 09:00 hrs and travelled to a town W, 255 km away, travelling at an average speed of 60 km h^{-1}. The time of arrival at town W was

  A 12:15 hrs   Ⓐ

  B 13:00 hrs   Ⓑ

  C 13:15 hrs   Ⓒ

  D 13:25 hrs   Ⓓ

8

EFGH is a trapezium such that EF = 8 cm, HG = 14 cm, and FH = 10 cm. The angles at E and H are right angles. The area of EFGH is

  A 66 cm^2 Ⓐ

  B 72 cm^2 Ⓑ

  C 84 cm^2 Ⓒ

  D 90 cm^2 Ⓓ

9

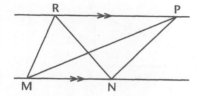

In the diagram above, the area of triangle MNR = x cm². The area of triangle MNP will be

A x cm²   Ⓐ

B $\frac{1}{2}x$ cm²   Ⓑ

C $\frac{1}{3}x$ cm²   Ⓒ

D $\frac{1}{4}x$ cm²   Ⓓ

10 A sum of money earns $72.00 simple interest at a rate of 6% annually for 2 years. The sum of money is

A $144.00   Ⓐ

B $600.00   Ⓑ

C $864.00   Ⓒ

D $7176.00   Ⓓ

11 A certain number is trebled and increased by 2. The result is 14. The number is

A 8   Ⓐ

B 6   Ⓑ

C 5   Ⓒ

D 4   Ⓓ

12 $\frac{2}{x} + \frac{3}{x}$ expressed as a single fraction is

A $\frac{5}{x^2}$ Ⓐ

B $\frac{6}{x^2}$ Ⓑ

C $\frac{5}{x}$ Ⓒ

D $\frac{6}{x}$ Ⓓ

13

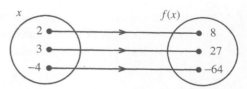

The mapping above may be written as

A $f(x) = \sqrt[3]{x}$ Ⓐ

B $f(x) = \dfrac{1}{\sqrt[3]{x}}$ Ⓑ

C $f(x) = x^3$ Ⓒ

D $f(x) = x^{-3}$ Ⓓ

14 If $2x + 1 > 9 + 4x$ then

A $x < -4$ Ⓐ

B $x > -4$ Ⓑ

C $x > 4$ Ⓒ

D $x < 4$ Ⓓ

15

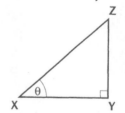

In the triangle above, $\cos(90 - \theta)$ is

A $\dfrac{YZ}{XZ}$ Ⓐ

B $\dfrac{XZ}{YZ}$ Ⓑ

C $\dfrac{XY}{XZ}$ Ⓒ

D $\dfrac{XZ}{XY}$ Ⓓ

16 From 12:30 pm to 12:45 pm, the hour hand of a clock rotates through

A 90°   Ⓐ

B 30°   Ⓑ

C 15°   Ⓒ

D $7\frac{1}{2}$°   Ⓓ

17 On a pie chart, a sector of angle $22\frac{1}{2}^\circ$ represents the portion of a field used to grow vegetables. As a fraction this is

A $\frac{1}{4}$ Ⓐ

B $\frac{1}{8}$ Ⓑ

C $\frac{1}{16}$ Ⓒ

D $\frac{1}{32}$ Ⓓ

18 A number x, is quadrupled and then the result is squared. This may be written as

A $4x^4$ Ⓐ

B $16x^2$ Ⓑ

C $4x^2$ Ⓒ

D $\dfrac{4}{x^2}$ Ⓓ

19 $(2x - 1)(3 - 5x) =$

A $11x + 10x^2 - 3$ Ⓐ

B $11x - 10x^2 - 3$ Ⓑ

C $-11x + 10x^2 + 3$ Ⓒ

D $-11x - 10x^2 + 3$ Ⓓ

20 $\dfrac{3}{x} = 1 + \frac{1}{4}$, then $x =$

A $\frac{12}{11}$ Ⓐ

B $\frac{12}{5}$ Ⓑ

C $\frac{11}{4}$ Ⓒ

D $\frac{11}{3}$ Ⓓ

21 In the number $14\,203_5$, the digit 2 represents

A 2×5^0 Ⓐ

B 2×5^1 Ⓑ

C 2×5^2 Ⓒ

D 2×5^3 Ⓓ

22

The figure above illustrates a triangle WXY with sides WX = 12 cm, XY = 5 cm, and WY = 13 cm. The triangle WXY is

A   right-angled   Ⓐ

B   acute-angled   Ⓑ

C   isosceles   Ⓒ

D   obtuse-angled   Ⓓ

23 If $X = \{$factors of $8\}$ and $Y = \{$factors of $16\}$, then

A $X \cap Y = \varnothing$ Ⓐ

B $X \subset Y$ Ⓑ

C $X \cup Y = X$ Ⓒ

D $Y \subset X$ Ⓓ

24 If x and y are positive integers and both x and y are odd, then xy will always be

A   odd   Ⓐ

B   even   Ⓑ

C   prime   Ⓒ

D   greater than 100   Ⓓ

25 If $R = \{$rectangles$\}$ and $P = \{$parallelograms$\}$, then

A $R = P$ Ⓐ

B $R \cap P = \varnothing$ Ⓑ

C $P \subset R$ Ⓒ

D $R \subset P$ Ⓓ

26

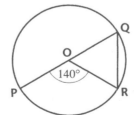

In the figure above, PQ is a diameter of the circle, centre O. R is a point on the

circumference and angle POR = 140°.
Angle OQR =

A 90° Ⓐ
B 70° Ⓑ
C 50° Ⓒ
D 40° Ⓓ

27 The point (2, −3) is reflected in the *x*-axis. The coordinates of the image are

A (2, 3) Ⓐ
B (−2, 3) Ⓑ
C (−2, −3) Ⓒ
D (−3, 2) Ⓓ

28 In a certain remote village of 625 people, 125 are infected with a virus. The probability that a randomly chosen villager is uninfected is

A $\frac{4}{5}$ Ⓐ

B $\frac{3}{5}$ Ⓑ

C $\frac{2}{5}$ Ⓒ

D $\frac{1}{5}$ Ⓓ

29 In a class of 80 students, each student studies at least one of the languages French or Spanish. If 40 students study French only and 30 study Spanish only, the number of students who study both is

A 40 Ⓐ
B 30 Ⓑ
C 20 Ⓒ
D 10 Ⓓ

30

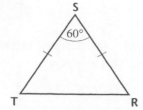

In the triangle RST, ST = SR and the angle TSR = 60°.

The triangle is

A scalene Ⓐ
B equilateral Ⓑ
C right-angled Ⓒ
D obtuse-angled Ⓓ

31

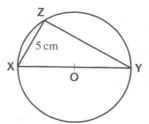

In the figure above, XY is a diameter of the circle, centre O and radius 6.5 cm. Z is a point on the circumference such that XZ = 5 cm. ZY =

A 5 cm Ⓐ
B 11.5 cm Ⓑ
C 12 cm Ⓒ
D 13 cm Ⓓ

32 5000 kg in tonnes is

A 0.5 tonnes Ⓐ
B 5 tonnes Ⓑ
C 50 tonnes Ⓒ
D 500 tonnes Ⓓ

33

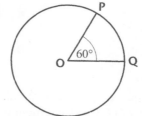

PQ is an arc of a circle, centre O, with ∠POQ = 60° as shown in the diagram. If the circumference of the circle is 38 cm, then the length of the major arc PQ is

A $\frac{1}{6} \times 38$ cm Ⓐ

B $\frac{1}{4} \times 38$ cm Ⓑ

C $\frac{3}{4} \times 38$ cm Ⓒ

D $\frac{5}{6} \times 38$ cm Ⓓ

34 Given $1.81 \times 0.34 = 0.6154$. The value of $181 \times 0.034 =$

A   0.061 54   Ⓐ
B   0.615 40   Ⓑ
C   6.154 00   Ⓒ
D   61.540 00   Ⓓ

35 The fractions $\frac{3}{7}$, $\frac{2}{9}$ and $\frac{4}{11}$ in ascending order of magnitude are

A $\frac{4}{11}, \frac{3}{7}, \frac{2}{9}$ Ⓐ
B $\frac{3}{7}, \frac{4}{11}, \frac{2}{9}$ Ⓑ
C $\frac{2}{9}, \frac{4}{11}, \frac{3}{7}$ Ⓒ
D $\frac{2}{9}, \frac{3}{7}, \frac{4}{11}$ Ⓓ

36 A shirt valued at $76.00 is given a $12\frac{1}{2}\%$ discount at a sale. The sale price is

A $88.50   Ⓐ
B $85.50   Ⓑ
C $66.50   Ⓒ
D $64.50   Ⓓ

37 If $1 US $\equiv$ $6.40 TT, then $153.60 TT in US dollars is

A $32.00 US   Ⓐ
B $28.50 US   Ⓑ
C $24.00 US   Ⓒ
D $22.25 US   Ⓓ

38 A sewing machine bought on hire purchase requires a deposit of $38.00 and monthly instalments of $18.00 over 2 years. The total cost of the machine is

A $470.00   Ⓐ
B $432.00   Ⓑ
C $254.00   Ⓒ
D $216.00   Ⓓ

39 An imported item bought for $800.00 requires a 30% duty and a 15% import tax. The final cost of the item is

A $920.00   Ⓐ
B $1040.00   Ⓑ
C $1120.00   Ⓒ
D $1160.00   Ⓓ

40 After 20% discount was given on a table, the sale price was $480.00. The price before the discount was

A $600.00   Ⓐ
B $540.00   Ⓑ
C $510.00   Ⓒ
D $490.00   Ⓓ

41 The quadrilateral has only one axis of symmetry as shown in the figure (not drawn to scale). The quadrilateral is a

A   rhombus   Ⓐ
B   kite   Ⓑ
C   parallelogram   Ⓒ
D   square   Ⓓ

42 In a certain school of 600 students, the probability that a randomly chosen student is a boy is $\frac{3}{5}$. The number of girls is

A   240   Ⓐ
B   360   Ⓑ
C   480   Ⓒ
D   520   Ⓓ

43 A man spends $\frac{1}{3}$ of $\frac{1}{2}$ his salary of $1200.00 on entertainment. This amounts to

A $100.00   Ⓐ
B $200.00   Ⓑ
C $400.00   Ⓒ
D $600.00   Ⓓ

44 (i)

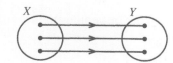

(ii)

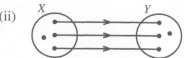

(iii)

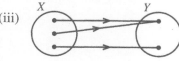

(iv)

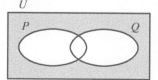

Which of the above diagrams does not represent a function?

A   (i)   Ⓐ
B   (ii)   Ⓑ
C   (iii)   Ⓒ
D   (iv)   Ⓓ

45 A girl spent $6.00 for lunch from her $10.00 allowance. 30% of the remainder she spent on sweets and gave her friend half of the rest. She now has

A $2.80   Ⓐ
B $1.40   Ⓑ
C $1.20   Ⓒ
D $0.80   Ⓓ

46 A man receives $810.00 after being taxed 10% of his salary. His gross salary is

A $891.00   Ⓐ
B $896.50   Ⓑ
C $900.00   Ⓒ
D $942.00   Ⓓ

47 A watch was bought by a store keeper for $480.00 and sold for $520.00. The percentage profit was

A $8\frac{1}{3}$ Ⓐ
B   12   Ⓑ
C $15\frac{1}{2}$ Ⓒ
D   40   Ⓓ

48 A driver left town P and drove for $3\frac{1}{4}$ hours. If he stopped for a 15 minute lunch break and arrived at his destination at 14:40 hours, his departure time from P was

A   12:00 hrs   Ⓐ
B   11:40 hrs   Ⓑ
C   11:25 hrs   Ⓒ
D   11:10 hrs   Ⓓ

49

The shaded region in the Venn diagram illustrates

A $P' \cap Q$ Ⓐ
B $P \cap Q$ Ⓑ
C $(P \cap Q)'$ Ⓒ
D $(P \cup Q)'$ Ⓓ

50 Given that $a * b$ denotes $\dfrac{a + 2b}{ab}$, then $(-3) * 2 =$

A $-\frac{1}{6}$ Ⓐ
B $-\frac{7}{8}$ Ⓑ
C $\frac{1}{6}$ Ⓒ
D $\frac{7}{6}$ Ⓓ

51 A block of wood in the shape of a cuboid has a height of $\frac{2}{3}x$ cm and length of $\frac{8}{3}x$ cm. If the volume of the block is $\frac{16x^3}{9}$ cm^3, then its width is

A $\frac{1}{4}x$ cm   Ⓐ
B $\frac{1}{2}x$ cm   Ⓑ
C $\frac{2}{3}x$ cm   Ⓒ
D x cm   Ⓓ

52 If $A = \{$prime numbers less than $10\}$, then $n(A) =$

   A 3   Ⓐ
   B 4   Ⓑ
   C 5   Ⓒ
   D 6   Ⓓ

53 Pens have to be shared among groups of 6, 8 or 12 boys. The least number of pens with which this can be done without any remainder is

   A 12   Ⓐ
   B 24   Ⓑ
   C 36   Ⓒ
   D 48   Ⓓ

54

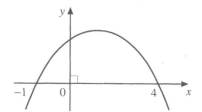

If the area of the above trapezium is 48 cm^2, then the value of x is

   A 11 cm   Ⓐ
   B 14 cm   Ⓑ
   C 16 cm   Ⓒ
   D 18 cm   Ⓓ

55 A fair coin and a fair die are tossed. The probability that the coin comes up 'heads' and the die shows a 'five' is

   A $\frac{1}{2}$ Ⓐ
   B $\frac{1}{6}$ Ⓑ
   C $\frac{1}{8}$ Ⓒ
   D $\frac{1}{12}$ Ⓓ

Questions 56–58 refer to the table below, showing the number of children in families living in a village.

Number of children	0	1	2	3	4	5	6
Number of families	8	15	30	41	32	12	12

56 The number of families in the village is

   A 42   Ⓐ
   B 100   Ⓑ
   C 150   Ⓒ
   D 180   Ⓓ

57 The median of the distribution is

   A 3   Ⓐ
   B 4   Ⓑ
   C 5   Ⓒ
   D 5.5   Ⓓ

58 A family is chosen at random. The probability of at least 4 children is

   A $\frac{16}{75}$ Ⓐ
   B $\frac{28}{75}$ Ⓑ
   C $\frac{47}{75}$ Ⓒ
   D $\frac{3}{4}$ Ⓓ

Questions 59–60 refer to the quadratic graph below.

59 The graph in the diagram can be represented by

   A $y = x^2 - 3x - 4$ Ⓐ
   B $y = x^2 - 3x + 4$ Ⓑ
   C $y = 3x - x^2 + 4$ Ⓒ
   D $y = -x^2 - 3x + 4$ Ⓓ

60 The range of values of x for which the function is negative is

   A $x \le 4$ and $x \ge -1$ Ⓐ
   B $x \ge 4$ or $x \le -1$ Ⓑ
   C $x < 4$ and $x > -1$ Ⓒ
   D $x > 4$ or $x < -1$ Ⓓ

Test number 8

Read the directions on page (iv) carefully.

1 $3x - 2(2x - 5) + 3(2 - 2x) =$

  A $16 - 7x$ Ⓐ
  B $-16 + 7x$ Ⓑ
  C $4 - 13x$ Ⓒ
  D $-4 + 13x$ Ⓓ

2 An item is purchased by making a down payment of $1152.00 and monthly instalments of $96.00 for n months. If the total cost of the item is $3456.00, then the value of n is

  A   48   Ⓐ
  B   36   Ⓑ
  C   24   Ⓒ
  D   12   Ⓓ

3 If $3 \begin{pmatrix} -2 \\ b \end{pmatrix} = \begin{pmatrix} -6 \\ -6 \end{pmatrix}$ then b is

  A -6 Ⓐ
  B -2 Ⓑ
  C   2   Ⓒ
  D   1   Ⓓ

4 The value of $3\frac{4}{7}$ to 2 significant figures is

  A   3.5   Ⓐ
  B   3.55   Ⓑ
  C   3.56   Ⓒ
  D   3.6   Ⓓ

5 The simple interest on $600.00 for 4 years at 3 per cent per annum is

  A $36.00   Ⓐ
  B $72.00   Ⓑ
  C $108.00   Ⓒ
  D $144.00   Ⓓ

Questions 6–8 are based on the information below.

A man leaves his house, H, at 11:15 hours and journeys for $3\frac{1}{2}$ hours to a town T. During this time he stopped for a 15 minute lunch break. His average speed was $60 \, \text{km h}^{-1}$.

6 The distance from H to T is

  A   180 km   Ⓐ
  B   195 km   Ⓑ
  C   210 km   Ⓒ
  D   225 km   Ⓓ

7 The time of arrival at T was

  A   15:00 hours   Ⓐ
  B   14:45 hours   Ⓑ
  C   14:30 hours   Ⓒ
  D   14:15 hours   Ⓓ

8 If he did not stop for lunch and his average speed remained the same, his time of arrival at T would have been

  A   14:15 hours   Ⓐ
  B   14:30 hours   Ⓑ
  C   14:45 hours   Ⓒ
  D   15:00 hours   Ⓓ

9

The set of values of x illustrated on the number line above is

A　$\{x: x < 4 \text{ and } x \geq -4\}$　Ⓐ
B　$\{x: x \leq 4 \text{ and } x > -4\}$　Ⓑ
C　$\{x: x < -4 \text{ or } x > 4\}$　Ⓒ
D　$\{x: x \leq -4 \text{ or } x > 4\}$　Ⓓ

10　$\sqrt{5184} =$

A　52　Ⓐ
B　62　Ⓑ
C　72　Ⓒ
D　82　Ⓓ

11　If $\dfrac{x}{3} - 2 = 4$, then $x =$

A　-18　Ⓐ
B　$\frac{1}{2}$　Ⓑ
C　6　Ⓒ
D　18　Ⓓ

12　At a sale an article is offered at $180.00. The original price was 20% more than this value. The percentage discount is

A　25%　Ⓐ
B　20%　Ⓑ
C　$16\frac{2}{3}\%$　Ⓒ
D　9%　Ⓓ

13

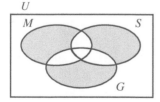

The Venn diagram above shows
$M = \{\text{Mathematics students}\}$,
$S = \{\text{Science students}\}$,
$G = \{\text{Geography students}\}$ in a class.
The shaded region represents

A　students who study all three subjects　Ⓐ
B　students who study two of the three subjects　Ⓑ
C　students who study one of these subjects　Ⓒ
D　students who study none of these subjects　Ⓓ

14　If $M = \begin{pmatrix} 1 & 2 \\ -1 & 1 \end{pmatrix}$ and $N = \begin{pmatrix} 2 & -2 \\ -1 & 3 \end{pmatrix}$ then $M - N =$

A　$\begin{pmatrix} -1 & 4 \\ -2 & -2 \end{pmatrix}$　Ⓐ

B　$\begin{pmatrix} 1 & -4 \\ 0 & 2 \end{pmatrix}$　Ⓑ

C　$\begin{pmatrix} -1 & 4 \\ 0 & -2 \end{pmatrix}$　Ⓒ

D　$\begin{pmatrix} 1 & 4 \\ 0 & -2 \end{pmatrix}$　Ⓓ

15　The angles of a triangle are in the ratio of $2:3:7$. The size of the smallest angle is

A　15°　Ⓐ
B　30°　Ⓑ
C　45°　Ⓒ
D　60°　Ⓓ

16　The mean of a set of 5 numbers is 3.6. If one of the numbers, 2, is removed, the mean of the remaining set of numbers is

A　4　Ⓐ
B　2　Ⓑ
C　1.6　Ⓒ
D　1.4　Ⓓ

17　If $n^n = 256$ then $n =$

A　12　Ⓐ
B　8　Ⓑ
C　4　Ⓒ
D　2　Ⓓ

18 If $\dfrac{2x}{0.125} = 0.5$ then $x =$

A $\dfrac{1}{32}$ Ⓐ

B $\dfrac{1}{16}$ Ⓑ

C $\dfrac{1}{8}$ Ⓒ

D $\dfrac{1}{4}$ Ⓓ

19 $\dfrac{x}{3} + \dfrac{3}{x} =$

A 1 Ⓐ

B $\dfrac{x^2 + 9}{3x}$ Ⓑ

C $\dfrac{x + 3}{9}$ Ⓒ

D $\dfrac{x^2 + 9}{9}$ Ⓓ

20 The point P $(-2, -4)$ is rotated through $180°$ about O to P$'$. The coordinates of P$'$ are

A $(-2, 4)$ Ⓐ

B $(2, -4)$ Ⓑ

C $(4, 2)$ Ⓒ

D $(2, 4)$ Ⓓ

21

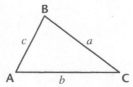

The area of the triangle ABC, shown above, is

A $bc \sin \angle A$ Ⓐ

B $\frac{1}{2}ac \sin \angle C$ Ⓑ

C $\frac{1}{2}(a + b + c)$ Ⓒ

D $\frac{1}{2}ab \sin \angle C$ Ⓓ

22 If $3x + 4y = 10$ and $-6x + by = -20$, then $b =$

A -8 Ⓐ

B -4 Ⓑ

C 4 Ⓒ

D 8 Ⓓ

23 If y is inversely proportional to the square of x and k is the constant of proportionality, then $y =$

A kx^2 Ⓐ

B $k\sqrt{x}$ Ⓑ

C $\dfrac{k}{x^2}$ Ⓒ

D $\dfrac{k}{\sqrt{x}}$ Ⓓ

24 If $\cos \angle A = \frac{5}{13}$ and $\angle A$ is reflex, then $\tan \angle A =$

A $\dfrac{12}{5}$ Ⓐ

B $\dfrac{5}{12}$ Ⓑ

C $-\dfrac{13}{12}$ Ⓒ

D $-\dfrac{12}{5}$ Ⓓ

25

P ——— 12 cm ——— Q
 5 cm
6 cm   R
 T   S

In the figure above, the area enclosed by PQRST is

A $87\,\text{cm}^2$ Ⓐ

B $84\,\text{cm}^2$ Ⓑ

C $72\,\text{cm}^2$ Ⓒ

D $40\,\text{cm}^2$ Ⓓ

26 $(a + b)^2 - (x + y)^2 =$

A $(a + b + x + y)(a - b - x - y)$ Ⓐ

B $(a + b + x + y)(a + b - x - y)$ Ⓑ

C $(a + b - x - y)(a - b - x + y)$ Ⓒ

D $(a + b - x - y)(a - b + x - y)$ Ⓓ

27 A number p is increased by 2, then doubled. The result squared can be expressed as

A $4(p + 2)^2$ Ⓐ

B $2(p + 2)^2$ Ⓑ

C $(2p + 2)^2$ Ⓒ

D $2p^2 + 2$ Ⓓ

28 If $a = 1$ and $b = 3$ then $\dfrac{a + 3b}{-ab} =$

  A $\dfrac{10}{3}$ Ⓐ

  B $\dfrac{3}{10}$ Ⓑ

  C $-\dfrac{3}{10}$ Ⓒ

  D $-\dfrac{10}{3}$ Ⓓ

29 If $a * b$ denotes $\dfrac{ab}{a + b}$ then $2 * 6 =$

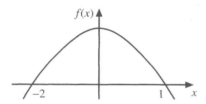

  A $\dfrac{13}{4}$ Ⓐ

  B $\dfrac{3}{2}$ Ⓑ

  C $\dfrac{2}{3}$ Ⓒ

  D $\dfrac{1}{3}$ Ⓓ

30

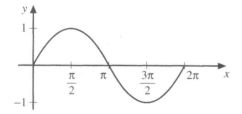

In the above quadratic, the values of x such that $f(x) > 0$ are

  A $x \geq 1$ or $x \leq -2$ Ⓐ

  B $x > 1$ or $x < 2$ Ⓑ

  C $x > -2$ and $x < 1$ Ⓒ

  D $x \geq -2$ and $x \leq -1$ Ⓓ

31

Which of the following could be represented by the above graph?

  A $y = \cos x$ Ⓐ

  B $y = \cos 2x$ Ⓑ

  C $y = \sin x$ Ⓒ

  D $y = \sin 2x$ Ⓓ

32 The interest on $1120.00 after $2\frac{1}{2}$ years is $196.00. The rate per annum is

  A   12%   Ⓐ

  B   8%   Ⓑ

  C   7%   Ⓒ

  D   6%   Ⓓ

33

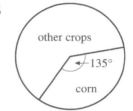

The above pie chart shows how a farmer divides his land. If the area used for growing corn is 12 hectares, then the area for other crops is

  A   16 hectares   Ⓐ

  B   20 hectares   Ⓑ

  C   32 hectares   Ⓒ

  D   36 hectares   Ⓓ

34

The circle is inscribed in a square of side 12 cm. The area of the circle is

  A $24\pi \, \text{cm}^2$ Ⓐ

  B $36\pi \, \text{cm}^2$ Ⓑ

  C $48\pi \, \text{cm}^2$ Ⓒ

  D $144\pi \, \text{cm}^2$ Ⓓ

35

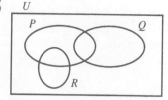

In the Venn diagram P, Q and R are sets. Which of the following statements are true?

I $P \cap Q \cap R \neq \varnothing$
II $R \subset Q$
III $P \cap Q = P \cap R$
IV $Q \cap R = \varnothing$

A   I, II and III only   Ⓐ
B   I and III only   Ⓑ
C   IV only   Ⓒ
D   None of the above   Ⓓ

36 The gradient of the line $\frac{2}{3}y = -x + 1$ is

A $\frac{3}{2}$ Ⓐ
B $\frac{2}{3}$ Ⓑ
C -1 Ⓒ
D $-\frac{3}{2}$ Ⓓ

37

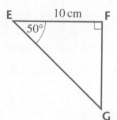

In the above triangle EFG, EF = 10 cm, $\angle$E = 50° and $\angle$F = 90°. The length of FG in cm is

A $10 \tan 50°$ Ⓐ
B $\dfrac{\tan 50°}{10}$ Ⓑ
C $10 \sin 50°$ Ⓒ
D $\dfrac{10}{\cos 50°}$ Ⓓ

38 123_4 written in base 8 is

A   27   Ⓐ
B   33   Ⓑ
C   246   Ⓒ
D   321   Ⓓ

39

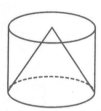

A cone is inscribed inside a cylinder so that it has the same base and same height. The ratio of the volume of the cone to that of the cylinder is

A $1:2$ Ⓐ
B $1:3$ Ⓑ
C $1:4$ Ⓒ
D $1:6$ Ⓓ

Questions 40–42 refer to the data below.

The heights of 10 trees in centimetres are 150, 155, 152, 153, 156, 160, 170, 165, 158, 155.

40 The median height is

A   158.0 cm   Ⓐ
B   156.0 cm   Ⓑ
C   155.0 cm   Ⓒ
D   155.5 cm   Ⓓ

41 The range of the distribution is

A   170 cm   Ⓐ
B   155.5 cm   Ⓑ
C   20 cm   Ⓒ
D   10 cm   Ⓓ

42 The mean height in cm is

A   157.4   Ⓐ
B   155.5   Ⓑ
C   150.0   Ⓒ
D   20.0   Ⓓ

43 $\sqrt{\dfrac{0.16}{6.25}} =$

A 0.16   (A)
B 0.625   (B)
C 1.6   (C)
D 2.5   (D)

44 $(p + q)^2 - 2pq =$

A $p^2 - q^2$ (A)
B $p^2 + q^2$ (B)
C $p^2 q^2$ (C)
D $p^2 + q^2 - 4pq$ (D)

45

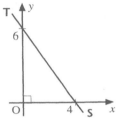

The gradient of the line ST, in the above diagram is

A $\dfrac{3}{2}$ (A)

B $\dfrac{2}{3}$ (B)

C $-\dfrac{2}{3}$ (C)

D $-\dfrac{3}{2}$ (D)

46 A regular polygon has interior angles that total 900°. If one side is 7 cm, then the perimeter of the polygon is

A 35 cm   (A)
B 49 cm   (B)
C 56 cm   (C)
D 63 cm   (D)

47 A rectangle is 3 times as long as it is wide. If its area is 27 cm² then its perimeter is

A 24 cm   (A)
B 36 cm   (B)
C 54 cm   (C)
D 81 cm   (D)

48 A triangle has sides that measure 8 cm, 10 cm and 10 cm. If all measurements are to the nearest cm, the least value of the perimeter is

A 17.0 cm   (A)
B 26.5 cm   (B)
C 29.0 cm   (C)
D 29.5 cm   (D)

49 $(2x - 3)^2 =$

A $2x^2 + 9$ (A)
B $2x^2 - 9$ (B)
C $4x^2 + 9$ (C)
D $4x^2 - 12x + 9$ (D)

50 If $f(x) = 2x + 1$, then $f(x^2) =$

A $4x^2 + 1$ (A)
B $(2x + 1)^2$ (B)
C $2x^2 + 1$ (C)
D $(4x + 1)^2$ (D)

Questions 51–54 are based on the table below.

Age of children	11	12	13	14	15	16
Number of children	6	3	5	4	4	3

The table shows the ages of children at a party.

51 The number of children at the party is

A 81   (A)
B 66   (B)
C 48   (C)
D 25   (D)

52 The modal age of the distribution is

A 6   (A)
B 9   (B)
C 11   (C)
D $13\frac{1}{2}$ (D)

53 The median age of the distribution is

   A 5   Ⓐ
   B 12   Ⓑ
   C 13   Ⓒ
   D $13\frac{1}{2}$ Ⓓ

54 The probability that a child chosen at random is at least 14 years old is

   A 0.16   Ⓐ
   B 0.28   Ⓑ
   C 0.44   Ⓒ
   D 0.56   Ⓓ

55

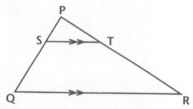

In the figure above PS = 2 cm, PQ = 6 cm and the area of triangle PST is 8 cm². If ST is parallel to QR then the area of QRTS is

   A 72 cm²   Ⓐ
   B 64 cm²   Ⓑ
   C 48 cm²   Ⓒ
   D 24 cm²   Ⓓ

56

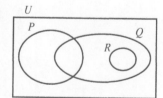

In the Venn diagram above, which of the statements about the sets P, Q and R are true?

  I $Q \subset R$
  II $P \cap R = \varnothing$
  III $Q \cap R = Q$
  IV $R \cup Q = Q$

   A I, II and III only   Ⓐ
   B I, II and IV only   Ⓑ
   C II, III and IV only   Ⓒ
   D II and IV only   Ⓓ

57 A man is four times as old as his son. In 6 years he will be three times as old. The son's present age is

   A 8 years   Ⓐ
   B 12 years   Ⓑ
   C 16 years   Ⓒ
   D 18 years   Ⓓ

58 A block of wood is in the shape of a cuboid of length x cm. Its width is $\frac{2}{3}$ of the length and the height is $\frac{3}{4}$ of the width. The volume of the block is

   A $\frac{1}{3}x^3$ cm³   Ⓐ
   B $\frac{2}{3}x^3$ cm³   Ⓑ
   C $\frac{3}{4}x^3$ cm³   Ⓒ
   D $2x^3$ cm³   Ⓓ

59 If $a = \begin{pmatrix} -3 \\ 3 \end{pmatrix}$, then $|2a| =$

   A $3\sqrt{2}$ units   Ⓐ
   B 6 units   Ⓑ
   C $6\sqrt{2}$ units   Ⓒ
   D 12 units   Ⓓ

60

W, X, Y and Z lie on the circumference of a circle. WT is the tangent at W and $\angle$YWT = 40°. If ZW = ZY, then $\angle$ZXW =

   A 50°   Ⓐ
   B 65°   Ⓑ
   C 70°   Ⓒ
   D 80°   Ⓓ

Test number 9

Read the directions on page (iv) carefully.

1 4.5 as a percentage of 1 is

   A   0.045%   (A)
   B   4.5%   (B)
   C   45%   (C)
   D   450%   (D)

2 In the number 3.082, the digit 8 represents

   A   8 thousandths   (A)
   B   8 hundredths   (B)
   C   8 tenths   (C)
   D   8 hundreds   (D)

3

In the above triangle, the value of $x°$ is

   A $30°$ (A)
   B $37\frac{1}{2}°$ (B)
   C $45°$ (C)
   D $60°$ (D)

4

4 cm

The surface area of the cube shown in the diagram is

   A $96\,cm^2$ (A)
   B $64\,cm^2$ (B)
   C $32\,cm^2$ (C)
   D $16\,cm^2$ (D)

5 The fractions $\frac{4}{7}$, $\frac{5}{9}$ and $\frac{3}{5}$ in ascending order of magnitude are

   A $\frac{3}{5}, \frac{5}{9}, \frac{4}{7}$ (A)
   B $\frac{5}{9}, \frac{4}{7}, \frac{3}{5}$ (B)
   C $\frac{3}{5}, \frac{4}{7}, \frac{5}{9}$ (C)
   D $\frac{5}{9}, \frac{3}{5}, \frac{4}{7}$ (D)

6 Sin θ is positive and cos θ negative for values of θ in

   A   quadrants I and II only   (A)
   B   quadrant III only   (B)
   C   quadrants III and IV only   (C)
   D   quadrant II only   (D)

7 If $f(x) = 2x + 1$, and $g(x) = x - 4$ then $gf(2) =$

   A -7 (A)
   B -3 (B)
   C 1 (C)
   D 5 (D)

8 An article originally priced at $80.00 was increased by 10%. At a sale the new price was reduced by 10%. The selling price of the article is now

   A $80.00   (A)
   B $79.20   (B)
   C $72.00   (C)
   D $64.00   (D)

9 $6x^2 + x - 2 =$

A $(6x - 1)(x + 2)$ Ⓐ

B $(6x + 1)(x - 2)$ Ⓑ

C $(2x + 1)(3x - 2)$ Ⓒ

D $(2x - 1)(3x + 2)$ Ⓓ

10 If $f:x \rightarrow \dfrac{3x - 1}{2}$, then $f^{-1}:x \rightarrow$

A $\dfrac{2x - 1}{3}$ Ⓐ

B $\dfrac{2x + 1}{3}$ Ⓑ

C $\dfrac{1 - 3x}{2}$ Ⓒ

D $\dfrac{1 + 3x}{-2}$ Ⓓ

11 The transformation matrix $\begin{pmatrix} -1 & 0 \\ 0 & -1 \end{pmatrix}$ represents

A 180° rotation about O   Ⓐ

B reflection in the line $y = -x$ Ⓑ

C rotation of −90° about O   Ⓒ

D reflection in the y-axis   Ⓓ

12 The number of axes of symmetry in a square is

A 1   Ⓐ

B 2   Ⓑ

C 3   Ⓒ

D 4   Ⓓ

13 U

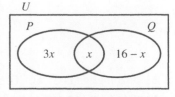

In the Venn diagram above, $n(P) = n(Q)$. The number of elements in P only is

A 4   Ⓐ

B 12   Ⓑ

C 16   Ⓒ

D 24   Ⓓ

14 Ben has twice as much money as his sister Jean. She has 3 times as much as Harry but only half as much as Janet. Together they have $32.00. Ben has

A $2.00   Ⓐ

B $6.00   Ⓑ

C $12.00   Ⓒ

D $14.00   Ⓓ

15 If $a * b$ denotes $(ba)^{ab}$ then $3 * 1 =$

A 3   Ⓐ

B 6   Ⓑ

C 9   Ⓒ

D 27   Ⓓ

16 A cellular telephone bill consists of a rental fee of $34.50 per month plus a fixed charge of $0.23 per minute for calls. If the bill at the end of a month was $82.80, the call time in minutes was

A 150   Ⓐ

B 210   Ⓑ

C 360   Ⓒ

D 400   Ⓓ

17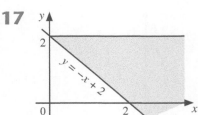

In the diagram above, the shaded region represents the set of points (x, y) for which

A $y \leq 2$ and $y \geq -x + 2$ Ⓐ

B $y \geq 2$ and $y \geq -x + 2$ Ⓑ

C $y \leq 2$ and $y \leq -x + 2$ Ⓒ

D $y \geq 2$ and $y \leq -x + 2$ Ⓓ

18 A reflection in the x-axis followed by a reflection in the y-axis is equivalent to

A a reflection in $y = -x$ Ⓐ
B a reflection in $y = x$ Ⓑ
C a rotation of 180° about O   Ⓒ
D a translation of $\begin{pmatrix} -1 \\ -1 \end{pmatrix}$ Ⓓ

19 The line $2y = 2x + 8$ cuts the x-axis at A and the y-axis at B. The area of triangle OAB is

A 4 square units   Ⓐ
B 8 square units   Ⓑ
C 16 square units   Ⓒ
D 32 square units   Ⓓ

20 In a cyclic quadrilateral, two opposite angles are in the ratio of $2 : 3$. The size of the smaller of these angles is

A 30°   Ⓐ
B 36°   Ⓑ
C 60°   Ⓒ
D 72°   Ⓓ

21

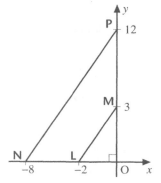

Triangle OLM is mapped onto triangle ONP by an enlargement

A centre O and scale factor 3   Ⓐ
B centre O and scale factor −3   Ⓑ
C centre O and scale factor 4   Ⓒ
D centre O and scale factor −4   Ⓓ

22 A fair die and a fair coin are tossed once each. The probability of getting a 'five' and a 'tail' is

A $\frac{2}{3}$ Ⓐ
B $\frac{1}{2}$ Ⓑ
C $\frac{5}{12}$ Ⓒ
D $\frac{1}{12}$ Ⓓ

23 $\sin^2 x = \frac{4}{9}$. The exact value of $\cos^2 x =$

A $-\frac{2}{3}$ Ⓐ
B $\frac{5}{9}$ Ⓑ
C $\frac{2}{3}$ Ⓒ
D 1   Ⓓ

24

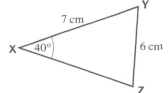

In the triangle above, $\sin \angle Z =$

A $\dfrac{6}{7 \sin 40°}$ Ⓐ
B $\dfrac{6 \sin 40°}{7}$ Ⓑ
C $\dfrac{7 \sin 40°}{6}$ Ⓒ
D $\dfrac{7}{6 \sin 40°}$ Ⓓ

25 The cost of $2\frac{1}{2}$ dozen eggs is \$7.50. The cost of $1\frac{1}{2}$ dozen eggs at the same rate is

A \$3.00   Ⓐ
B \$4.50   Ⓑ
C \$5.75   Ⓒ
D \$6.25   Ⓓ

26 $\dfrac{2x}{3} - \dfrac{3}{2x} =$

A   0   (A)

B $\dfrac{2x - 3}{3 - 2x}$ (B)

C $\dfrac{4x^2 - 9}{6x}$ (C)

D $\dfrac{9 - 4x^2}{6x}$ (D)

27 A container holds $56\,000\ \text{cm}^3$ of water. This volume expressed in litres is

A   0.56   (A)
B   5.6   (B)
C   56   (C)
D   560   (D)

28

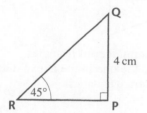

In the triangle above, $\angle R = 45°$ and $PQ = 4$ cm. $QR =$

A $\dfrac{1}{4\sqrt{2}}$ cm   (A)

B $\dfrac{\sqrt{2}}{4}$ cm   (B)

C $\dfrac{4}{\sqrt{2}}$ cm   (C)

D $4\sqrt{2}$ cm   (D)

29 0.000 501 in standard form is

A 5.01×10^{-3} (A)
B 5.01×10^{-4} (B)
C 5.01×10^{-5} (C)
D 5.01×10^{-6} (D)

30 In the set of numbers 32, 17, 14, −2, 8, 3, the smallest and largest numbers are deleted. The mean of the remaining numbers is

A   7.0   (A)
B   10.5   (B)
C   12.0   (C)
D   18.0   (D)

31 A man buys an article and sells it for $4.80, making a profit of 20%. If his profit had to be 25%, his selling price would have been

A $4.85   (A)
B $4.95   (B)
C $5.00   (C)
D $6.00   (D)

32 If $s = ut + \frac{1}{2}at^2$ then $a =$

A $\dfrac{2(s - ut)}{t^2}$ (A)

B $\dfrac{s - ut}{2t^2}$ (B)

C $\dfrac{ut - s}{2t^2}$ (C)

D $\dfrac{2(ut - s)}{t^2}$ (D)

33 Given $\sqrt{18.5} = 4.3$, then the value of $\sqrt{0.001\,85} =$

A 4.3×10^{-4} (A)
B 4.3×10^{-2} (B)
C 4.3×10^{2} (C)
D 4.3×10^{4} (D)

34 If x is an integer and $-2 < x - 1 < 2$ then the set of values of x is

A $\{-3, -2, -1, 0, 1, 2, 3\}$ (A)
B $\{-2, -1, 0, 1, 2\}$ (B)
C $\{0, 1, 2\}$ (C)
D $\{-3, -2, -1, 0\}$ (D)

35

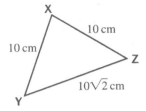

In the triangle XYZ, XY = XZ = 10 cm and YZ = $10\sqrt{2}$ cm. The following statements have been made:

I the triangle is right-angled
II the triangle is isosceles
III sin $\angle$XYZ = cos $\angle$XZY

The true statements are

A I and II only Ⓐ
B II and III only Ⓑ
C I and III only Ⓒ
D I, II and III Ⓓ

36 If $\dfrac{x^2}{y} = \dfrac{y^2}{x}$ then

A $x^3 = y$ Ⓐ
B $x = y^3$ Ⓑ
C $y = x$ Ⓒ
D $\dfrac{y^2}{x} = \dfrac{y}{x^2}$ Ⓓ

37 The curve $x^2 + y^2 + 2x - 3y - 6 = 0$ passes through

A $(-1, -2)$ Ⓐ
B $(1, 2)$ Ⓑ
C $(-1, 2)$ Ⓒ
D $(2, 1)$ Ⓓ

38 10010_2 expressed in base 10 is

A 34 Ⓐ
B 18 Ⓑ
C 11 Ⓒ
D 8 Ⓓ

39 $(x + 1)$ is not a factor of

A $x^2 + 3x + 2$ Ⓐ
B $x^2 - 1$ Ⓑ
C $x^2 + x + 1$ Ⓒ
D $2x^2 + x - 1$ Ⓓ

40 Which of the following is not rational?

A $\sqrt{8}$ Ⓐ
B $\sqrt[3]{64}$ Ⓑ
C $\sqrt[5]{32}$ Ⓒ
D $\sqrt[3]{\dfrac{27}{8}}$ Ⓓ

41 Which of the following is the best estimate for $\dfrac{\sqrt{3.94} \times 24.97}{10.14}$?

A 0.05 Ⓐ
B 0.5 Ⓑ
C 5 Ⓒ
D 50 Ⓓ

42

The smallest number of triangles, congruent to the one in the above diagram, needed to form a square is

A 2 Ⓐ
B 4 Ⓑ
C 8 Ⓒ
D 16 Ⓓ

43

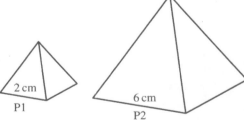

P1 and P2 are 2 similar square pyramids with corresponding base sides of 2 cm and 6 cm respectively. The ratio of the volumes of P1 to P2 is

A 1 : 27 Ⓐ
B 1 : 9 Ⓑ
C 1 : 3 Ⓒ
D 1 : 2 Ⓓ

44 The point P (−1, 3) is mapped onto P′ by a −90° rotation about O. The coordinates of P′ are

A   (3, 1)   (A)
B   (3, −1)   (B)
C   (−1, −3)   (C)
D   (1, −3)   (D)

45 10% of 10% of 1 in standard form is

A 1×10^2 (A)
B 1×10 (B)
C 1×10^{-1} (C)
D 1×10^{-2} (D)

46

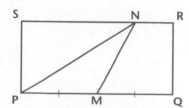

PQRS is a rectangle. M is the midpoint of PQ and N is a point on SR. The ratio of the area of triangle PMN to the area of rectangle PQRS is

A   1 : 2   (A)
B   1 : 4   (B)
C   1 : 6   (C)
D   1 : 8   (D)

Questions 47–50 refer to the diagram below.

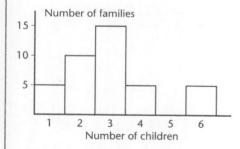

The above diagram shows the number of children in the families that live in a small village.

47 The total number of children in the families is

A   120   (A)
B   100   (B)
C   30   (C)
D   21   (D)

48 The mean number of children per family is

A   6   (A)
B   5   (B)
C   4   (C)
D   3   (D)

49 The modal number of children per family is

A   6   (A)
B   5   (B)
C   3   (C)
D   1   (D)

50 The probability that a family, chosen at random has less than 4 children is

A $\frac{1}{8}$ (A)
B $\frac{1}{4}$ (B)
C $\frac{3}{4}$ (C)
D $\frac{7}{8}$ (D)

51 Two fair dice are tossed once each. The probability of a total score of 5 is

A $\frac{1}{9}$ (A)
B $\frac{1}{6}$ (B)
C $\frac{1}{3}$ (C)
D $\frac{5}{12}$ (D)

53 After an importer paid 30% of the cost of an item in taxes and $65.00 in freight charges, the total bill was $520.00. The cost price of the item was

A $455.00   (A)
B $390.00   (B)
C $350.00   (C)
D $221.00   (D)

53 The interquartile range of the set of numbers 7, 9, 13, 15, 17, 12 and 10 is

A   10   Ⓐ
B   6   Ⓑ
C   5   Ⓒ
D   3   Ⓓ

54 A rectangular plot of land measures 800 m by 900 m. The area in hectares is

A   7200   Ⓐ
B   720   Ⓑ
C   72   Ⓒ
D   7.2   Ⓓ

55

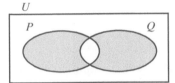

In the Venn diagram above, the shaded region represents

A $P' \cap Q$ Ⓐ
B $(P \cap Q') \cup (Q \cap P')$ Ⓑ
C $(P \cup Q)'$ Ⓒ
D $(P \cap Q)'$ Ⓓ

56

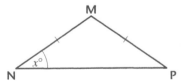

In the triangle MNP, $\angle M > 100°$. Then $x°$

A $< 40°$ Ⓐ
B $> 80°$ Ⓑ
C $= 80°$ Ⓒ
D $= 40°$ Ⓓ

57 A bag contains only red balls, yellow balls and green balls. There are 30 balls in the bag. The probability of drawing a red ball is $\frac{2}{5}$ and there are as many yellow balls as green balls. The number of green balls is

A   6   Ⓐ
B   9   Ⓑ
C   12   Ⓒ
D   18   Ⓓ

58 If $1.00 EC ≡ $3.00 TT and $1.00 EC ≡ $0.50 US, then $90.00 TT in $US is

A $15.00 US   Ⓐ
B $30.00 US   Ⓑ
C $45.00 US   Ⓒ
D $60.00 US   Ⓓ

59 $\dfrac{x^2 + x - 6}{x^2 - 3x + 2} =$

A $\dfrac{x - 6}{-3x + 2}$ Ⓐ

B $\dfrac{x + 3}{x - 1}$ Ⓑ

C $\dfrac{x + 3}{x - 2}$ Ⓒ

D $\dfrac{x - 3}{x + 1}$ Ⓓ

60 The ordered pair (x, y) that satisfies the equations $3x + y = 5$ and $2x + 3y - 1 = 0$ is

A $(2, 2)$ Ⓐ
B $(-2, -1)$ Ⓑ
C $(1, 2)$ Ⓒ
D $(2, -1)$ Ⓓ

Test number ⑩

Read the directions on page (iv) carefully.

1 The decimal equivalent of $\frac{15}{8}$ is

A   0.533   Ⓐ
B   1.625   Ⓑ
C   1.875   Ⓒ
D   1.933   Ⓓ

2 $(-2a)^2 \times (a)^{-3} =$

A $4a^5$ Ⓐ

B $\dfrac{a}{4}$ Ⓑ

C $\dfrac{4}{a}$ Ⓒ

D $4a$ Ⓓ

3 The size of each exterior angle of a regular hexagon is

A   30°   Ⓐ
B   60°   Ⓑ
C   90°   Ⓒ
D   120°   Ⓓ

4 From 2:15 am to 2:45 am the hour hand of a clock rotates through an angle of

A   15°   Ⓐ
B   30°   Ⓑ
C   90°   Ⓒ
D   180°   Ⓓ

5 In a given distribution the difference between the smallest and the largest values is

A   range   Ⓐ
B   mode   Ⓑ
C   median   Ⓒ
D   mean   Ⓓ

6 $(1.2 \times 10^3) \times (1.2 \times 10^{-5}) =$

A 1.2×10^{-2} Ⓐ
B 1.2×10^8 Ⓑ
C 1.44×10^{-2} Ⓒ
D 1.44×10^8 Ⓓ

7 If $U = \{\text{quadrilaterals}\}$, $P = \{\text{parallelograms}\}$, $R = \{\text{rectangles}\}$

I

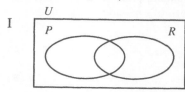

II

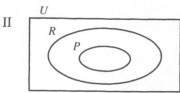

III

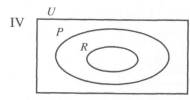

IV

The diagram which illustrates the relationship between U, P and R is

A   I   Ⓐ
B   II   Ⓑ
C   III   Ⓒ
D   IV   Ⓓ

8

POQ is a diameter of a circle, centre O, and R is a point on the circumference. If $\angle POR = 110°$ then $\angle ORQ =$

A 60°   Ⓐ
B 55°   Ⓑ
C 45°   Ⓒ
D 35°   Ⓓ

9 The volume of a pyramid is $64\,cm^3$. If the base is square and the height is 12 cm, then the length of one side of the base is

A $\dfrac{4}{\sqrt{3}}\,cm$ Ⓐ

B $4\,cm$ Ⓑ

C $5\frac{1}{3}\,cm$ Ⓒ

D $6\,cm$ Ⓓ

10 $4\pi^2 - 9e^2 =$

A $(4\pi - 9e)(\pi + e)$ Ⓐ
B $(2\pi - 3e)(2\pi - 3e)$ Ⓑ
C $(2\pi - 3e)(2\pi + 3e)$ Ⓒ
D $(4\pi - e)(\pi - 9e)$ Ⓓ

11

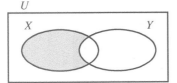

In the Venn diagram, the shaded region represents

A $Y' \cap X$ Ⓐ
B $(X \cap Y)'$ Ⓑ
C $X' \cap Y'$ Ⓒ
D $(X \cup Y)'$ Ⓓ

12 If $3 - 2x < 2x - 1$, then

A $x < \frac{1}{2}$ Ⓐ

B $x > \frac{1}{2}$ Ⓑ

C $x < 1$ Ⓒ

D $x > 1$ Ⓓ

13

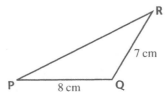

If the area of triangle PQR is $14\,cm^2$ and $\angle Q$ is obtuse, then $\angle Q =$

A 120°   Ⓐ
B 130°   Ⓑ
C 150°   Ⓒ
D 160°   Ⓓ

14 A particular shirt was available in two different shops at the same price. At sale time one shop offers a 20% discount, for $64.00. The other offers only a 10% discount. The sale price in the second shop was

A $69.12   Ⓐ
B $72.00   Ⓑ
C $76.80   Ⓒ
D $80.00   Ⓓ

15 The diagonals of a rhombus are 10 cm and 24 cm. The side of the rhombus in cm is

A 18   Ⓐ
B 17   Ⓑ
C 14   Ⓒ
D 13   Ⓓ

16 For which of the following functions is $f(2) = 7$?

A $f(x) = \dfrac{3 + 2x}{x}$ Ⓐ

B $f(x) = x^3 + 2$ Ⓑ

C $f(x) = x^2 - 3x + 2$ Ⓒ

D $f(x) = 2x^2 - x + 1$ Ⓓ

17 If $\tan \angle A = \frac{8}{15}$ and $\angle A$ is reflex, then $\sin \angle A =$

A $-\dfrac{15}{17}$ Ⓐ

B $-\dfrac{8}{17}$ Ⓑ

C $\dfrac{8}{17}$ Ⓒ

D $\dfrac{15}{17}$ Ⓓ

18 The curve $y = x^2 + 2x - 3$ cuts the x-axis at

A $x = 1$ and 3 Ⓐ

B $x = -1$ and -3 Ⓑ

C $x = -1$ and 3 Ⓒ

D $x = 1$ and -3 Ⓓ

19

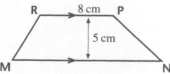

In the trapezium MNPR, MN is parallel to RP and the perpendicular distance between them is 5 cm. If RP = 8 cm and the area of MNPR is 65 cm², then MN =

A   13 cm   Ⓐ

B $15\frac{1}{2}$ cm   Ⓑ

C   18 cm   Ⓒ

D   20 cm   Ⓓ

20 $X = \begin{pmatrix} 3x & 4 \\ -1 & 2y \end{pmatrix}$ and $Y = \begin{pmatrix} -6 & 4 \\ -1 & 1 \end{pmatrix}$.

If $X = Y$ then the value of x and of y is

A $x = -2$ and $y = \frac{1}{2}$ Ⓐ

B $x = 2$ and $y = \frac{1}{2}$ Ⓑ

C $x = 2$ and $y = -\frac{1}{2}$ Ⓒ

D $x = -2$ and $y = -\frac{1}{2}$ Ⓓ

21

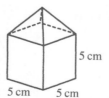

The figure above shows a solid block of wood in the shape of a cube of side 5 cm with a pyramid of height 3 cm at one end as shown in the diagram. The volume of the solid is

A   125 cm³   Ⓐ

B   150 cm³   Ⓑ

C   175 cm³   Ⓒ

D   200 cm³   Ⓓ

22 The area of the largest possible square inscribed in a rectangle 16 cm long and 9 cm wide is

A   36 cm²   Ⓐ

B   72 cm²   Ⓑ

C   81 cm²   Ⓒ

D   256 cm²   Ⓓ

23

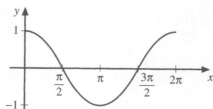

Which of the following functions may be represented by the above graph?

A $y = \sin x$ Ⓐ

B $y = \cos x$ Ⓑ

C $y = \tan x$ Ⓒ

D $y = \sin x + \cos x$ Ⓓ

24 If $-k\begin{pmatrix} a \\ b \end{pmatrix} = \begin{pmatrix} 3a \\ 3b \end{pmatrix}$, then $k =$

A   3   Ⓐ

B $\frac{1}{3}$ Ⓑ

C $-\frac{1}{3}$ Ⓒ

D -3 Ⓓ

25 If $62_{10} \equiv 222_n$, then n is

A   2   (A)
B   4   (B)
C   5   (C)
D   6   (D)

26

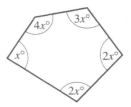

In the above polygon, the size of x is

A   15   (A)
B   30   (B)
C   45   (C)
D   60   (D)

27 The transformation matrix that represents an enlargement, centre origin and scale factor 2 is

A $\begin{pmatrix} 0 & 2 \\ 2 & 0 \end{pmatrix}$ (A)

B $\begin{pmatrix} 0 & -2 \\ -2 & 0 \end{pmatrix}$ (B)

C $\begin{pmatrix} 2 & 0 \\ 0 & 1 \end{pmatrix}$ (C)

D $\begin{pmatrix} 2 & 0 \\ 0 & 2 \end{pmatrix}$ (D)

28 $2^6 \div 4^{-2} =$

A 2^{10} (A)
B 2^8 (B)
C 2^2 (C)
D 2^{-3} (D)

29 If $\dfrac{x}{3} - 2 = \dfrac{x}{2} + 3$ then $x =$

A -5 (A)
B -25 (B)
C -30 (C)
D -36 (D)

30

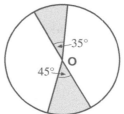

In the above circle, centre O, the unshaded regions represent a fraction of the circle of

A $\dfrac{4}{5}$ (A)

B $\dfrac{7}{9}$ (B)

C $\dfrac{1}{2}$ (C)

D $\dfrac{2}{9}$ (D)

31 A set of cards is numbered from 1 to 20. The probability that a card picked at random has a prime number is

A $\dfrac{8}{19}$ (A)

B $\dfrac{2}{5}$ (B)

C $\dfrac{9}{20}$ (C)

D $\dfrac{1}{2}$ (D)

32 Which of the following sets of numbers does not have an HCF of 2 and LCM of 60?

A   {4, 6, 10}   (A)
B   {10, 20, 30}   (B)
C   {2, 30, 60}   (C)
D   {2, 20, 120}   (D)

33 If $1\frac{1}{2} : 2\frac{1}{2} = 3\frac{1}{2} : x$, then x is

A $4\frac{1}{2}$ Ⓐ

B $5\frac{5}{6}$ Ⓑ

C $6\frac{1}{2}$ Ⓒ

D 7   Ⓓ

34

Allowance	Amount per year
Personal	$2 000.00
Wife	$1 000.00
Child	$500.00
Mortgage interest	≤ $10 000.00

The above table shows the tax allowances allowed for a man who works for $4000.00 per month, pays mortgage interest of $16 000.00, has a wife and 4 children. His taxable income per year is

A $33 000.00   Ⓐ
B $27 000.00   Ⓑ
C $21 000.00   Ⓒ
D $15 000.00   Ⓓ

35 If $7 * 28 = 3$ then $a * b$ may be denoted by

A $ab - 1$ Ⓐ

B $\dfrac{2b}{a} + 1$ Ⓑ

C a^b Ⓒ

D $\dfrac{b}{a} - 1$ Ⓓ

36

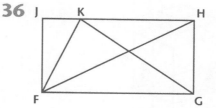

FGHJ is a rectangle and K is a point on JH. The ratio of the area of triangle FKG to the area of triangle FHG is

A $1 : 2$ Ⓐ
B $2 : 1$ Ⓑ
C $1 : 1$ Ⓒ
D $1 : 4$ Ⓓ

37 A fair die is tossed. It is tossed again until a number obtained before is observed again. The maximum number of tosses that is necessary to get a number twice is

A 7   Ⓐ
B 6   Ⓑ
C 4   Ⓒ
D 2   Ⓓ

38 $(a + b)^2 - (a^2 + b^2) =$

A 0   Ⓐ
B $2ab$ Ⓑ
C $2a^2 - 2b^2$ Ⓒ
D $a^2 b^2$ Ⓓ

39 The volume of a piece of metal alloy is 3 cm^3 and its mass is 8.1 g. The density of the metal in g cm^{-3} is

A   2.7   Ⓐ
B   5.1   Ⓑ
C   11.1   Ⓒ
D   24.3   Ⓓ

40

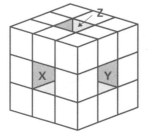

The diagram above shows a large cube of side 6 cm made up of cubes of side 2 cm placed together. Square holes of side 2 cm are drilled through X, Y and Z, as shown in the diagram, to the opposite faces. The volume of the remaining solid is

A 144 cm^3 Ⓐ
B 160 cm^3 Ⓑ
C 168 cm^3 Ⓒ
D 182 cm^3 Ⓓ

41

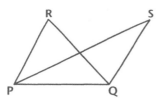

The triangles PQR and PQS have the same area. Which of the statements is true?

A   They are congruent.   Ⓐ
B   They are similar.   Ⓑ
C   They are equilateral.   Ⓒ
D   They have the same height.   Ⓓ

42   A boy buys plums at 2 for 60¢ and mangoes at 2 for 90¢. If he buys the same number of plums as mangoes and spends a total of $12.00, then the number of fruits bought is

A   8   Ⓐ
B   16   Ⓑ
C   32   Ⓒ
D   64   Ⓓ

43   In a regular octagon, the size of each exterior angle is

A $22\frac{1}{2}°$ Ⓐ
B   45°   Ⓑ
C   90°   Ⓒ
D   135°   Ⓓ

44   The table below shows how a company calculates the electricity bill. Use the table to answer question 44.

Electricity 'units' used	Charge
≤ 500 units	20¢ each
> 500 units	30¢ each
10% on total charges – Government Tax	

If a previous reading was 3214 units and the present reading is 5124 units, then the bill will be

A $477.50   Ⓐ
B $523.00   Ⓑ
C $525.25   Ⓒ
D $575.30   Ⓓ

45   A salesman receives 8% commission on his sales plus a base salary of $120.00 per week. If a particular week's salary totalled $344.00, his sales amounted to

A $2800.00   Ⓐ
B $2912.00   Ⓑ
C $4300.00   Ⓒ
D $4487.00   Ⓓ

46   A virus has infected one in seven children in a town. If 420 are not infected, then the population of children is

A   427   Ⓐ
B   480   Ⓑ
C   490   Ⓒ
D   2940   Ⓓ

47 $0.01 \times 1.001 =$

A 100.1 Ⓐ
B 0.100 1 Ⓑ
C 0.010 01 Ⓒ
D 0.001 001 Ⓓ

48

MNPR is a rectangle and S is the midpoint of RP. The ratio of the area of triangle MRS to the area of triangle MSN is

A 2 : 1 Ⓐ
B 1 : 1 Ⓑ
C 1 : 2 Ⓒ
D 1 : 3 Ⓓ

49 If $f(x) = 3x + 2$, and $g(x) = x^2$, then $fg(x) =$

A $(3x + 2)^2$ Ⓐ
B $3x^2 + 2$ Ⓑ
C $(3x)^2 + 2$ Ⓒ
D $(3x)^2 + 2^2$ Ⓓ

Questions 50–53 refer to the table below showing the number of chickens on some farms.

Number of chickens	200	250	300	350	400	500
Number of farms	4	2	3	6	2	3

50 The total number of chickens on the farms surveyed is

A 2 000 Ⓐ
B 2 100 Ⓑ
C 6 600 Ⓒ
D 10 000 Ⓓ

51 The median of the distribution is

A 350 Ⓐ
B 325 Ⓑ
C 300 Ⓒ
D 150 Ⓓ

52 The mean number of chickens per farm is

A 300 Ⓐ
B 325 Ⓑ
C 330 Ⓒ
D 350 Ⓓ

53 If a farm is chosen at random, the probability that it has at most 300 chickens is

A $\frac{9}{20}$ Ⓐ
B $\frac{11}{20}$ Ⓑ
C $\frac{3}{5}$ Ⓒ
D $\frac{7}{10}$ Ⓓ

54 The algebraic statement $n - m^3$ may be expressed as

A the cube of m diminished by n Ⓐ
B n increased by the cube of m Ⓑ
C the cube of n diminished by m Ⓒ
D n decreased by the cube of m Ⓓ

55 A man, X, runs twice the distance run by another man Y. X takes one half the time taken by Y. The ratio of the speed of X to the speed of Y is

A 4 : 1 Ⓐ
B 2 : 1 Ⓑ
C 1 : 1 Ⓒ
D 1 : 4 Ⓓ

56

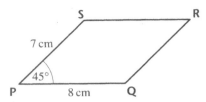

PQRS is a parallelogram with PQ = 8 cm, PS = 7 cm and angle SPQ = 45°. The area of triangle PQR is

A $14\sqrt{2}\,\text{cm}^2$ Ⓐ

B $28\,\text{cm}^2$ Ⓑ

C $56\,\text{cm}^2$ Ⓒ

D $56\sqrt{2}\,\text{cm}^2$ Ⓓ

57

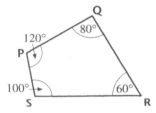

The quadrilateral PQRS can be described as

A   a trapezium   Ⓐ

B   a kite   Ⓑ

C   cyclic   Ⓒ

D   symmetrical about PR   Ⓓ

58   The sum of the ages of two boys, Mark and John is 34 and the difference is 2. If Mark is the younger boy, John's age is

A   15 years   Ⓐ

B   16 years   Ⓑ

C   17 years   Ⓒ

D   18 years   Ⓓ

59

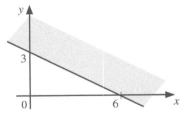

The shaded region illustrates

A $2y + x - 6 \le 0$ Ⓐ

B $x + 2y + 6 \le 0$ Ⓑ

C $x - 2y + 6 \ge 0$ Ⓒ

D $2y + x - 6 \ge 0$ Ⓓ

60

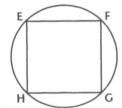

EFGH is the largest possible square inscribed in a circle of radius 4 cm. The area of the square is

A $16\,\text{cm}^2$ Ⓐ

B $16\sqrt{2}\,\text{cm}^2$ Ⓑ

C $32\,\text{cm}^2$ Ⓒ

D $32\sqrt{2}\,\text{cm}^2$ Ⓓ

Test number 11

Read the directions on page (iv) carefully.

1 $\sqrt[3]{8a^3b^{-6}} =$

   A $2ab^{-3}$ Ⓐ

   B $2ab^{-2}$ Ⓑ

   C $2\frac{2}{3}ab^{-2}$ Ⓒ

   D $8ab^{-3}$ Ⓓ

2   In 4.5×10^{-3}, the value of the 4 is

   A   4 units   Ⓐ

   B   4 tenths   Ⓑ

   C   4 hundredths   Ⓒ

   D   4 thousandths   Ⓓ

3 $\dfrac{0.10 \times 1.01}{0.01} =$

   A   0.101   Ⓐ

   B   1.01   Ⓑ

   C   10.1   Ⓒ

   D   101.0   Ⓓ

4   If $-3(x-1) + 2(1-x) > 0$, then

   A $x < 1$ Ⓐ

   B $x > 1$ Ⓑ

   C $x < -1$ Ⓒ

   D $x > -1$ Ⓓ

5   A salesman receives a basic salary of $80.00 per week plus commission. In a particular week he received a total of $224.00 from sales amounting to $3600.00.

His commission was

   A   4%   Ⓐ

   B $6\frac{2}{9}\%$ Ⓑ

   C $8\frac{4}{9}\%$ Ⓒ

   D $10\frac{1}{2}\%$ Ⓓ

6   Which of the following numbers written to 3 decimal places and 3 significant figures is the same?

   A   8.3714   Ⓐ

   B   3.3333   Ⓑ

   C   0.4781   Ⓒ

   D   0.0066   Ⓓ

7   A boat travelling west changes course by turning 135° anticlockwise. The bearing of the new direction is

   A   045°   Ⓐ

   B   135°   Ⓑ

   C   180°   Ⓒ

   D   225°   Ⓓ

8   One fourth of the people in a town are infected with a virus X, and one fifth of the remainder with virus Y. The fraction of the population that is not infected by either virus X or virus Y is

   A $\frac{3}{20}$ Ⓐ

   B $\frac{2}{5}$ Ⓑ

   C $\frac{9}{20}$ Ⓒ

   D $\frac{3}{5}$ Ⓓ

9 From 3 o'clock to 6 o'clock the minute hand of a clock rotates through an angle of

A   45°   Ⓐ
B   360°   Ⓑ
C   1080°   Ⓒ
D   1200°   Ⓓ

10 Ann and Mary share $121.00 with Mary getting $33.00 more than Ann. The ratio of Ann's share to Mary's share is

A $11:3$ Ⓐ
B $3:11$ Ⓑ
C $4:7$ Ⓒ
D $1:2$ Ⓓ

11 A hollow cuboid is of dimensions 4 cm by 5 cm by 6 cm. The volume of the largest possible cube that could fit into this cuboid is

A $216\,cm^3$ Ⓐ
B $125\,cm^3$ Ⓑ
C $120\,cm^3$ Ⓒ
D $64\,cm^3$ Ⓓ

12 If $S = \{odd\ numbers\}$, $T = \{even\ numbers\}$ then the Venn diagram which illustrates the relationship between S and T is

A 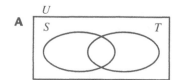 Ⓐ

B 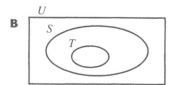 Ⓑ

C 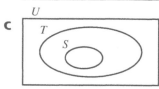 Ⓒ

D Ⓓ

13 $1.2 \times 10^{-3} + 1.8 \times 10^{-3}$ in standard form is

A 2.16×10^{-6} Ⓐ
B 3.0×10^{-6} Ⓑ
C 3.0×10^{-3} Ⓒ
D 3.0×10^{9} Ⓓ

14 A sum of $4000.00 invested for 3 years at 5% per annum simple interest will amount to

A $600.00   Ⓐ
B $3400.00   Ⓑ
C $4600.00   Ⓒ
D $5000.00   Ⓓ

15 $\dfrac{2.4 \times 10^{-1}}{0.12 \times 10^{-2}} =$

A   0.2   Ⓐ
B   2   Ⓑ
C   20   Ⓒ
D   200   Ⓓ

16 The marks by 15 students in a test are 14, 6, 6, 10, 11, 14, 18, 20, 11, 14, 13, 8, 8, 14, 13. The modal score is

A   12   Ⓐ
B   14   Ⓑ
C   15   Ⓒ
D   20   Ⓓ

17 $a^2 = b^2 + c^2 - 2bc \cos A$, so $\cos A =$

A $\dfrac{a^2 - b^2 - c^2}{2bc}$ Ⓐ

B $\dfrac{b^2 + c^2 - a^2}{2bc}$ Ⓑ

C $\dfrac{b^2 + c^2 - a^2}{-2bc}$ Ⓒ

D $\dfrac{a^2 + b^2 + c^2}{2bc}$ Ⓓ

18 If $P = \{x: -2 < x < 5;\ x \in Z\}$ and $Q = \{x: -5 < x < 2;\ x \in Z\}$ then $P \cap Q =$

A $\{-5, -4, \ldots, 4, 5\}$ Ⓐ
B $\{-1, 0, 1, 2\}$ Ⓑ
C $\{-1, 0, 1\}$ Ⓒ
D $\varnothing$ Ⓓ

19 $\dfrac{1}{\sqrt[3]{\dfrac{8}{27}}} =$

A $\dfrac{27}{8}$ (A)

B $\dfrac{3}{2}$ (B)

C $\dfrac{2}{3}$ (C)

D $-\dfrac{3}{2}$ (D)

20 If $a = \begin{pmatrix} -3 \\ -2 \end{pmatrix}$ and $b = \begin{pmatrix} 7 \\ 4 \end{pmatrix}$, then $\frac{1}{2}(a + b) =$

A $\begin{pmatrix} 2 \\ 1 \end{pmatrix}$ (A)

B $\begin{pmatrix} 5 \\ 3 \end{pmatrix}$ (B)

C $\begin{pmatrix} 4 \\ 2 \end{pmatrix}$ (C)

D $\begin{pmatrix} -5 \\ -3 \end{pmatrix}$ (D)

21 The cube of a number n is squared. This statement can be expressed algebraically as

A $\sqrt[3]{n^2}$ (A)

B $(n^2)^2$ (B)

C $\sqrt{n^3}$ (C)

D $(n^3)^2$ (D)

22

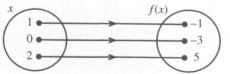

The above diagram illustrates the function

A $f{:}x \rightarrow 2x - 3$ (A)

B $f{:}x \rightarrow x^2 - 3$ (B)

C $f{:}x \rightarrow 2x + 5$ (C)

D $f{:}x \rightarrow 2x^2 - 3$ (D)

23 At a sale a pair of shoes cost $45.00 after a 10% discount. If the shop had offered a 20% discount, the cost would have been

A $40.00   (A)

B $36.00   (B)

C $35.00   (C)

D $25.00   (D)

24 If $f{:}x \rightarrow 4x - 1$ and $g{:}x \rightarrow x^2$ then $gf{:}x \rightarrow$

A $4x^2 - 1$ (A)

B $4x^2 + 1$ (B)

C $(4x - 1)^2$ (C)

D $4(x - 1)^2$ (D)

25 $U = \{$Members of a club$\}$
$H = \{$Members who play Hockey$\}$
$C = \{$Members who play Cricket$\}$
$F = \{$Members who play Football$\}$

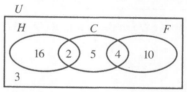

The probability that a member from the club chosen at random plays hockey only **or** cricket and football is

A $\dfrac{1}{2}$ (A)

B $\dfrac{31}{40}$ (B)

C $\dfrac{7}{8}$ (C)

D $\dfrac{37}{40}$ (D)

26 A man has twin sons. He is twice as old as they are. The sum of all their ages is 100. How old are the sons?

A 15 years   (A)

B 20 years   (B)

C 25 years   (C)

D 30 years   (D)

27 The number of tonnes in 1 kilogram is

   A   1000   Ⓐ
   B   100   Ⓑ
   C   0.01   Ⓒ
   D   0.001   Ⓓ

28 Sin 60° ≡

   A   1   Ⓐ

   B $\dfrac{\sqrt{3}}{2}$ Ⓑ

   C $\frac{1}{2}$ Ⓒ

   D $\dfrac{2}{\sqrt{3}}$ Ⓓ

29

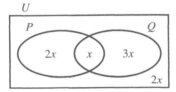

In the above Venn diagram, $n(U) = 32$, $n(P) =$

   A   4   Ⓐ
   B   8   Ⓑ
   C   12   Ⓒ
   D   16   Ⓓ

30

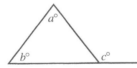

An equation relating $a°$, $b°$ and $c°$ is

   A $c° + a° + b° = 180°$ Ⓐ
   B $c° = a° + b°$ Ⓑ
   C $a° = b° - c°$ Ⓒ
   D $a° + b° = 180° + c°$ Ⓓ

31 The compound interest after 2 years on $400.00 at 5% per annum is

   A $100.00   Ⓐ
   B $50.00   Ⓑ
   C $41.00   Ⓒ
   D $40.00   Ⓓ

32 A farmer grows three crops, carrots, peas, and corn. He uses 40% of his land for carrots and divides the rest to peas and corn in the ratio 1 : 5. On a pie chart, the angle of the sector representing peas is

   A   144°   Ⓐ
   B   120°   Ⓑ
   C   60°   Ⓒ
   D   36°   Ⓓ

33

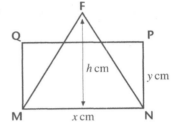

MNPQ is a rectangle of length x cm and width y cm. The height of triangle MNF is h cm. If the triangle and rectangle have the same area, then

   A $h = 2y$ Ⓐ
   B $h = y$ Ⓑ
   C $h = \frac{1}{2}y^2$ Ⓒ
   D $h = \frac{1}{2}y$ Ⓓ

34 $U = \{$cars$\}$, $S = \{$sports cars$\}$ and $R = \{$red sports cars$\}$.

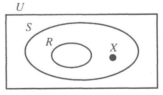

The car, X, as shown in the Venn diagram is

   A   a red sports car   Ⓐ
   B   a car that is not red and is not a sports car   Ⓑ
   C   a red car that is not a sports car   Ⓒ
   D   a sports car that is not red   Ⓓ

35 If $3:5 = 4:x$ then $x =$

A $2\frac{1}{2}$ Ⓐ

B 6 Ⓑ

C $6\frac{2}{3}$ Ⓒ

D 8 Ⓓ

36 A tank in the shape of a cuboid measures 2 metres long, 1 metre wide and 1 metre high. Its volume in cm^3 is

A 2×10^8 Ⓐ

B 2×10^6 Ⓑ

C 2×10^3 Ⓒ

D 2×10^2 Ⓓ

37

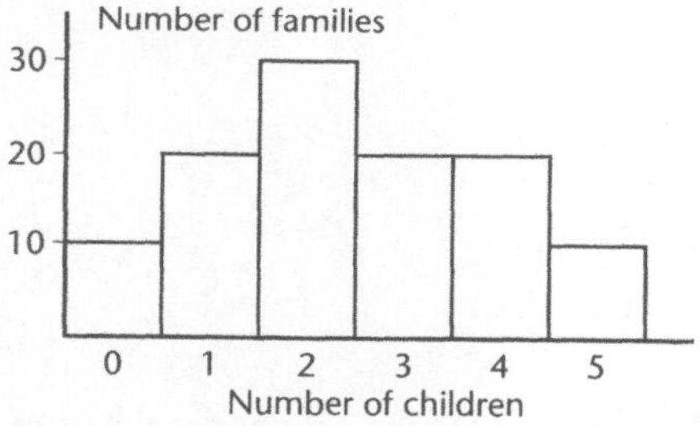

The diagram above shows the number of children in the families of a neighbourhood. The number of families in the neighbourhood is

A   30 Ⓐ

B   100 Ⓑ

C   110 Ⓒ

D   270 Ⓓ

38 An item discounted by 15% cost $170.00. The original cost of the item was

A $181.33 Ⓐ

B $185.00 Ⓑ

C $195.50 Ⓒ

D $200.00 Ⓓ

39 The point (3, 2) is reflected in the line l to produce an image (7, 2). The equation of the line l is

A $x = 2$ Ⓐ

B $y = 2$ Ⓑ

C $x = 5$ Ⓒ

D $y = 5$ Ⓓ

40 The interest rate on a deposit of $8000.00 was increased from 8% to $8\frac{3}{4}$%. The difference in interest is

A $60.00 Ⓐ

B $50.00 Ⓑ

C $40.00 Ⓒ

D $30.00 Ⓓ

41 A pair of shoes priced at $240.00 is allowed a $12\frac{1}{2}$% discount at a sale. The shoes will now cost

A $30.00 Ⓐ

B $210.00 Ⓑ

C $228.50 Ⓒ

D $252.50 Ⓓ

42 If $H = \{x: 1 < x < 4, x \in Z\}$ then $n(H) =$

A   1 Ⓐ

B   2 Ⓑ

C   3 Ⓒ

D   4 Ⓓ

43

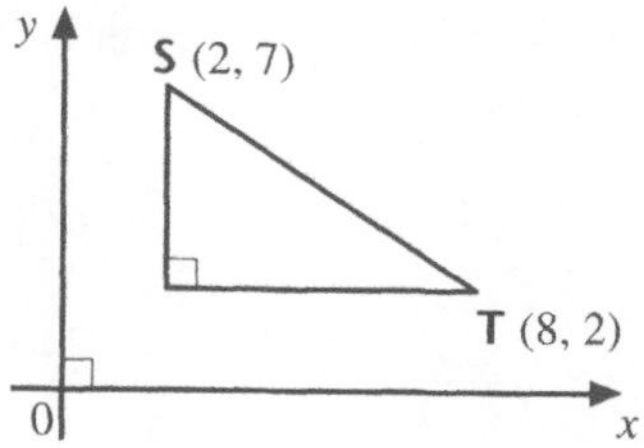

In the diagram above, the gradient of the line ST is

A $\frac{6}{5}$ Ⓐ

B $\frac{5}{6}$ Ⓑ

C $-\frac{6}{5}$ Ⓒ

D $-\frac{5}{6}$ Ⓓ

44 A circle and a square have the same area. If the square is of side 4 cm, then the radius of the circle is

A $\dfrac{16}{\sqrt{\pi}}$ Ⓐ

B $\dfrac{8}{\sqrt{\pi}}$ Ⓑ

C $\dfrac{4}{\sqrt{\pi}}$ Ⓒ

D $\dfrac{2}{\sqrt{\pi}}$ Ⓓ

45 The ages of two men M and N are in the ratio 3 : 5. If the difference in their ages is 18 years, then the age of N is

A   45 years   Ⓐ
B   27 years   Ⓑ
C   18 years   Ⓒ
D   9 years   Ⓓ

46

Number of children

The diagram shows the amount of allowance money received by children in a class. The mode of the distribution is

A   12   Ⓐ
B   9   Ⓑ
C   8   Ⓒ
D   5   Ⓓ

47 A plot of land valued at $80 000 appreciates by 10% after one year. It appreciates by a further 5% during the second year. Its value after 2 years is

A $87 500.00   Ⓐ
B $92 000.00   Ⓑ
C $92 400.00   Ⓒ
D $95 000.00   Ⓓ

48 In the sector, the length of arc $PQ = \frac{1}{2}r$. The angle θ in radians is

A $\frac{1}{4}$ Ⓐ
B $\frac{1}{2}$ Ⓑ
C   1   Ⓒ
D   2   Ⓓ

49 The matrix that represents an enlargement, centre O and scale factor 3 is

A $\begin{pmatrix} 0 & 3 \\ 3 & 0 \end{pmatrix}$ Ⓐ

B $\begin{pmatrix} 0 & \frac{1}{3} \\ \frac{1}{3} & 0 \end{pmatrix}$ Ⓑ

C $\begin{pmatrix} 3 & 1 \\ 1 & 3 \end{pmatrix}$ Ⓒ

D $\begin{pmatrix} 3 & 0 \\ 0 & 3 \end{pmatrix}$ Ⓓ

50 If $a * b$ denotes the remainder when ab is divided by 5, then $7 * 4$ is

A   1   Ⓐ
B   2   Ⓑ
C   3   Ⓒ
D   4   Ⓓ

51 $\dfrac{\pi^2 - 9}{\pi + 3} =$

A $\pi - 3$ Ⓐ
B $\pi + 3$ Ⓑ
C $\pi^2 - 3$ Ⓒ
D $\pi^2 + 3$ Ⓓ

52 If $\dfrac{4}{x^2} + 1 = 17$ and $x > 0$, then $x =$

A   2   Ⓐ
B $\frac{1}{2}$ Ⓑ
C $\frac{1}{4}$ Ⓒ
D $\frac{1}{16}$ Ⓓ

53 The area of a sector is $2r^2$ square units, where the radius of the circle is r units. The angle θ in radians is

A $\frac{1}{2}$ Ⓐ
B 1   Ⓑ
C 2   Ⓒ
D 4   Ⓓ

54 A fair die is tossed and comes up '4'. It is tossed a second time. The probability of '4' occurring again is

A $\frac{1}{36}$ Ⓐ
B $\frac{1}{6}$ Ⓑ
C $\frac{1}{3}$ Ⓒ
D $\frac{2}{3}$ Ⓓ

55

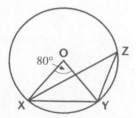

X, Y and Z are points on the circumference of a circle, centre O and ∠XOY = 80°. ∠XZY =

A 100°   Ⓐ
B 90°   Ⓑ
C 80°   Ⓒ
D 40°   Ⓓ

56 $A = \frac{1}{2}r^2\theta$ then $r =$

A $\sqrt{\dfrac{2A}{\theta}}$ Ⓐ

B $\sqrt{\dfrac{\theta}{2A}}$ Ⓑ

C $\sqrt{\dfrac{A}{2\theta}}$ Ⓒ

D $\sqrt{\dfrac{2\theta}{A}}$ Ⓓ

57

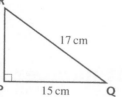

In the right-angled triangle above, PQ = 15 cm and QR = 17 cm. The perimeter of PQR is

A 60 cm   Ⓐ
B 40 cm   Ⓑ
C 34 cm   Ⓒ
D 32 cm   Ⓓ

58 The sum of the interior angles of a polygon is 900°. The number of sides of the polygon is

A 5   Ⓐ
B 6   Ⓑ
C 7   Ⓒ
D 8   Ⓓ

59 The graph of $y = x^2 - 4x - 5$ has axis of symmetry

A $x = -2$ Ⓐ
B $x = 2$ Ⓑ
C $y = -2$ Ⓒ
D $y = 2$ Ⓓ

60 $y = 2x - 3$ and $2y - 3x + 4 = 0$ are two lines, which meet at

A (−3, 4)   Ⓐ
B (4, −3)   Ⓑ
C (3, −4)   Ⓒ
D (2, 1)   Ⓓ

Test number ⑫

Read the directions on page (iv) carefully.

1 $15x^2y - 20xy = 5xy \times N$. Therefore N is

  A $\quad 4y - 3x$ Ⓐ

  B $\quad 3y - 4x$ Ⓑ

  C $\quad 3x - 4$ Ⓒ

  D $\quad 4x - 3y$ Ⓓ

2 $\left(\dfrac{27}{8}\right)^{-\frac{1}{3}} =$

  A $\quad \dfrac{2}{3}$ Ⓐ

  B $\quad \dfrac{8}{9}$ Ⓑ

  C $\quad \dfrac{9}{8}$ Ⓒ

  D $\quad \dfrac{3}{2}$ Ⓓ

3 Of the following fractions, the best approximation to $\dfrac{1}{\pi}$ is

  A $\quad \dfrac{3}{1}$ Ⓐ

  B $\quad \dfrac{1}{2}$ Ⓑ

  C $\quad \dfrac{1}{3}$ Ⓒ

  D $\quad \dfrac{1}{4}$ Ⓓ

4 If $f\colon x \to 3x - 5$, then $f^{-1}\colon x \to$

  A $\quad \dfrac{3}{x+5}$ Ⓐ

  B $\quad \dfrac{x+5}{3}$ Ⓑ

  C $\quad \frac{1}{3}x + 5$ Ⓒ

  D $\quad \frac{1}{3}x - 5$ Ⓓ

5 The exact value of $\sin 45°$ is

  A $\quad \dfrac{1}{\sqrt{2}}$ Ⓐ

  B $\quad \dfrac{\sqrt{3}}{2}$ Ⓑ

  C $\quad \dfrac{2}{\sqrt{3}}$ Ⓒ

  D $\quad \sqrt{2}$ Ⓓ

6 The number of solutions in the quadratic equation $3x^2 - 11x - 4 = 0$ is

  A $\quad 0$ Ⓐ

  B $\quad 1$ Ⓑ

  C $\quad 2$ Ⓒ

  D $\quad 3$ Ⓓ

7 If $\overrightarrow{AB} = \begin{pmatrix} 2 \\ 3 \end{pmatrix}$ and $\overrightarrow{BC} = \begin{pmatrix} 4 \\ 6 \end{pmatrix}$ then the ratio $|\overrightarrow{AB}| : |\overrightarrow{AC}|$ is

  A $\quad 1 : 1$ Ⓐ

  B $\quad 1 : 2$ Ⓑ

  C $\quad 1 : 3$ Ⓒ

  D $\quad 1 : 4$ Ⓓ

8 The transformation matrix $\begin{pmatrix} 0 & -1 \\ -1 & 0 \end{pmatrix}$ represents

  A   rotation of $90°$ about O   Ⓐ

  B   rotation of $-90°$ about O   Ⓑ

  C   reflection in the x-axis   Ⓒ

  D   reflection in the line $y = -x$ Ⓓ

9 A piece of string 120 cm long is cut in 2 pieces with one piece 20 cm longer than the other. The ratio of the shorter to the longer piece of string is

A   1 : 6   Ⓐ
B   1 : 5   Ⓑ
C   2 : 5   Ⓒ
D   5 : 7   Ⓓ

10 $1\frac{1}{7} + 2\frac{2}{3} =$

A $\frac{17}{21}$ Ⓐ
B $2\frac{17}{21}$ Ⓑ
C $3\frac{2}{10}$ Ⓒ
D $3\frac{17}{21}$ Ⓓ

11 A tank has a rectangular base of size 8 m by 6 m. The area of its base is

A $4.8 \times 10 \, \text{cm}^2$ Ⓐ
B $4.8 \times 10^2 \, \text{cm}^2$ Ⓑ
C $4.8 \times 10^4 \, \text{cm}^2$ Ⓒ
D $4.8 \times 10^5 \, \text{cm}^2$ Ⓓ

12 The number of litres in 1 ml is

A   0.001   Ⓐ
B   0.1   Ⓑ
C   10   Ⓒ
D   1000   Ⓓ

Questions 13–14 are based on the table below.

The table below shows the marks made by 90 students in a test marked out of 24.

Number of marks	0–4	5–9	10–14	15–19	20–24
Frequency	18	42	27	10	3

13 The modal class is

A   20–24   Ⓐ
B   10–14   Ⓑ
C   5–9   Ⓒ
D   0–4   Ⓓ

14 The probability that a student chosen at random obtained a mark of at least 15 but no more than 19 is

A $\frac{87}{90}$ Ⓐ
B $\frac{17}{45}$ Ⓑ
C $\frac{13}{90}$ Ⓒ
D $\frac{1}{9}$ Ⓓ

15

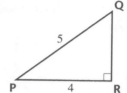

In the above triangle, the value of sin P tan P =

A $\frac{20}{9}$ Ⓐ
B $\frac{5}{4}$ Ⓑ
C $\frac{4}{5}$ Ⓒ
D $\frac{9}{20}$ Ⓓ

16 If $\dfrac{P}{S} + 1 = r$, then S is

A $\dfrac{P}{r-1}$ Ⓐ

B $\dfrac{r-1}{P}$ Ⓑ

C $\dfrac{r+1}{P}$ Ⓒ

D $\dfrac{P}{r+1}$ Ⓓ

17 $4a^2 - 1 =$

A $(1 - 2a)(1 + 2a)$ Ⓐ
B $(2a - 1)(2a - 1)$ Ⓑ
C $(2a - 1)(2a + 1)$ Ⓒ
D $(4a - 1)(a + 1)$ Ⓓ

18 160 degrees is equivalent to

A $\dfrac{16\pi}{9}$ radians   Ⓐ

B $\dfrac{8\pi}{9}$ radians   Ⓑ

C $\dfrac{4\pi}{9}$ radians   Ⓒ

D $\dfrac{9\pi}{16}$ radians   Ⓓ

19 If $a * b$ denotes the positive square root of ab, then $(4 * 9) * 24 =$

A 4   Ⓐ
B 6   Ⓑ
C 12   Ⓒ
D 18   Ⓓ

20 The region $\{(x, y): x \geq 5\}$ is illustrated by

A 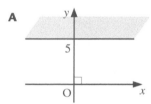   Ⓐ

B 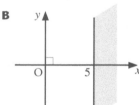   Ⓑ

C 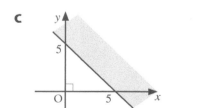   Ⓒ

D 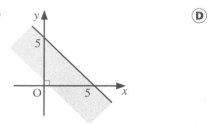   Ⓓ

21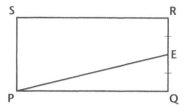

PQRS is a rectangle and E is the midpoint of QR. The ratio of the area of triangle PQE to the area of trapezium PSRE is

A $1:1$ Ⓐ
B $1:2$ Ⓑ
C $1:3$ Ⓒ
D $1:4$ Ⓓ

22 $\dfrac{a}{\sin A} = \dfrac{c}{\sin C}$ so sin C =

A $\dfrac{ac}{\sin A}$ Ⓐ

B $\dfrac{c \sin A}{a}$ Ⓑ

C $\dfrac{a \sin A}{c}$ Ⓒ

D $\dfrac{\sin A}{ac}$ Ⓓ

23 If R is the radius of the earth, then the radius of the circle of latitude 80° North is

A R sin 80°   Ⓐ

B $\dfrac{R}{\sin 80°}$ Ⓑ

C R cos 80°   Ⓒ

D $\dfrac{R}{\cos 80°}$ Ⓓ

24 Any two circles with the same centre are said to be

A orthogonal   Ⓐ
B equivalent   Ⓑ
C great   Ⓒ
D concentric   Ⓓ

25 If p is inversely proportional to q, then which of the following figures illustrates the relationship between p and q?

A 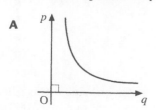   Ⓐ

B 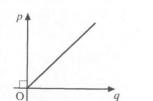   Ⓑ

C 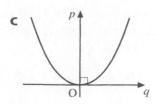   Ⓒ

D 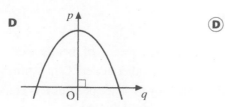   Ⓓ

26 Which of the following is irrational?

A $\dfrac{\pi}{3}$ Ⓐ

B $\sqrt{9}$ Ⓑ

C $\sin 30°$ Ⓒ

D $\sqrt[3]{8}$ Ⓓ

27 If x is an integer and $\{x: x > 2\} \cap \{x: x < -2\}$ then $x =$

A $\{-2, -1, 0, 1, 2\}$ Ⓐ
B $\{-1, 0, 1\}$ Ⓑ
C $\{3, 4, \ldots\}$ Ⓒ
D $\{\ \}$ Ⓓ

28 If $12\frac{1}{2}\%$ of x is 12.5 then x is

A 156.25   Ⓐ
B 100.0   Ⓑ
C 10.0   Ⓒ
D 1.0   Ⓓ

29 A man bought an article at a sale for 20% off the marked price. Later he sold the article for 20% more than he paid. His selling price compared to the marked price of the article was

A more   Ⓐ
B less   Ⓑ
C same   Ⓒ
D More information is required   Ⓓ
       to make this deduction.

30

Company rental of meter	$18 per month
First 10 000 litres	1¢ per litre
After the first 10 000 litres	$1\frac{1}{2}$¢ per litre
Government Tax on total	10%

The above chart shows the water charges for a household. During a particular month a family used 15 000 litres of water. Their monthly bill will be

A $267.30   Ⓐ
B $212.30   Ⓑ
C $193.00   Ⓒ
D $168.00   Ⓓ

31 Five squares of area 25 cm² each are placed together so as to form the figure shown in the diagram. The perimeter of the figure shown is

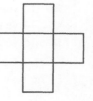

A 100 cm   Ⓐ
B 80 cm   Ⓑ
C 60 cm   Ⓒ
D 20 cm   Ⓓ

32 If $T = 2\pi\sqrt{\dfrac{m}{k}}$ then $k =$

A $\dfrac{4\pi^2 m}{T^2}$ Ⓐ

B $\dfrac{T^2}{4\pi^2 m}$ Ⓑ

C $\dfrac{T^2}{2\pi\sqrt{m}}$ Ⓒ

D $\dfrac{4\pi^2 T}{m^2}$ Ⓓ

33 In a football competition teams get 3 points for a win, 1 point for a draw and 0 points for a loss. After 4 matches a team has 5 points. The number of draws in these 4 matches must be

A 0   Ⓐ
B 1   Ⓑ
C 2   Ⓒ
D 3   Ⓓ

34 A bullet travels at $400\,\text{m s}^{-1}$. Its speed in km h^{-1} is

A   24   Ⓐ
B $111\frac{1}{9}$ Ⓑ
C   1440   Ⓒ
D   4000   Ⓓ

35 A boy and his sister's ages are in the ratio $6 : 7$. She is 2 years older than he is. The boy's age is

A 12 years   Ⓐ
B 13 years   Ⓑ
C 14 years   Ⓒ
D 15 years   Ⓓ

36 If $\dfrac{2x}{3y} = \dfrac{V}{9y}$ then $V =$

A $6xy$ Ⓐ
B $6x$ Ⓑ
C $6y$ Ⓒ
D 6   Ⓓ

37 The area of the largest circle that can be inscribed in a square of side 14 cm is

A $88\,\text{cm}^2$ Ⓐ
B $154\,\text{cm}^2$ Ⓑ
C $196\,\text{cm}^2$ Ⓒ
D $616\,\text{cm}^2$ Ⓓ

38 An empty cubic tank of side 6 m is filled with water at a constant rate of $12\,000\,\text{cm}^3$ per second. The tank will fill in

A 0.5 hours   Ⓐ
B 1.08 hours   Ⓑ
C 5.0 hours   Ⓒ
D 10.8 hours   Ⓓ

39 An article X, when reduced by $12\frac{1}{2}\%$ costs twice as much as article Y which costs $35.00. The cost of X is

A $70.00   Ⓐ
B $80.00   Ⓑ
C $87.50   Ⓒ
D $280.00   Ⓓ

40 An athlete, P, covers $\frac{2}{3}$ of the distance covered by another athlete Q in $\frac{2}{3}$ times the time taken by Q. The speed of P is equal to the speed of Q multiplied by

A $\frac{4}{9}$ Ⓐ
B 1   Ⓑ
C $\frac{4}{3}$ Ⓒ
D $\frac{9}{4}$ Ⓓ

41 A bag has 10 marbles of which half are green. Two marbles are chosen without replacement. The probability that both are green is

A $\frac{1}{5}$ Ⓐ
B $\frac{2}{9}$ Ⓑ
C $\frac{1}{4}$ Ⓒ
D $\frac{1}{2}$ Ⓓ

42

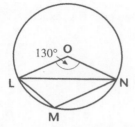

In the figure above, not drawn to scale, L, M and N are points on the circumference of a circle, centre O. If $\angle LON = 130°$, then $\angle LMN =$

A   90°   Ⓐ
B   100°   Ⓑ
C   115°   Ⓒ
D   130°   Ⓓ

43   The number 40_8 written in base 10 is

A   50   Ⓐ
B   48   Ⓑ
C   42   Ⓒ
D   32   Ⓓ

44   A straight line passes through the points (0, 2) and (2, 0). Its equation is

A $y = -x + 2$ Ⓐ
B $y = 2x$ Ⓑ
C $y = 2x + 2$ Ⓒ
D $y = 2x - 2$ Ⓓ

45   A number n is doubled; the result is cubed and then increased by 2. This statement may be represented algebraically by

A $2n^3 + 2$ Ⓐ
B $(2n)^3 + 2$ Ⓑ
C $(3n)^2 + 2$ Ⓒ
D $(2n + 2)^3$ Ⓓ

46   If $a = 2$, $b = 1$ and $c = -1$, then $\left(\dfrac{a}{b}\right)^c =$

A -2 Ⓐ
B $-\dfrac{1}{2}$ Ⓑ
C $\dfrac{1}{2}$ Ⓒ
D   2   Ⓓ

47   A set of scores is arranged in order of magnitude. The middle score is called the

A   range   Ⓐ
B   mode   Ⓑ
C   median   Ⓒ
D   mean   Ⓓ

Questions 48–49 refer to the diagram shown.

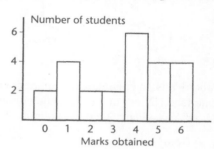

The above diagram shows the marks obtained by students in a test.

48   The number of students who sat the test is

A   21   Ⓐ
B   22   Ⓑ
C   24   Ⓒ
D   36   Ⓓ

49   The probability that a student chosen at random from the class scores 2 or 6 marks is

A $\dfrac{1}{2}$ Ⓐ
B $\dfrac{1}{3}$ Ⓑ
C $\dfrac{1}{4}$ Ⓒ
D $\dfrac{1}{12}$ Ⓓ

50   A bag contains 8 mangoes and n oranges. The probability of choosing a mango from the bag is $\frac{2}{3}$. The number of oranges is

A   16   Ⓐ
B   12   Ⓑ
C   8   Ⓒ
D   4   Ⓓ

51 If $ax^2 - 28x + 49$ is a perfect square then $a =$

A   21   Ⓐ
B   7   Ⓑ
C   4   Ⓒ
D   2   Ⓓ

52

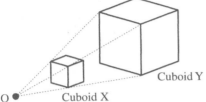

Cuboid Y
O ● Cuboid X

Cuboid Y is an enlargement, centre O and scale factor 2, of cuboid X. If the volume of cuboid Y is 48 cm^3, then the volume of X is

A   6 cm^3 Ⓐ
B   12 cm^3 Ⓑ
C   16 cm^3 Ⓒ
D   24 cm^3 Ⓓ

53 The transformation matrix $\begin{pmatrix} 1 & 0 \\ 0 & -1 \end{pmatrix}$ represents a reflection in

A   the x-axis   Ⓐ
B   the line $y = x$ Ⓑ
C   the line $y = -x$ Ⓒ
D   the y-axis   Ⓓ

54 If $2x - 1 < x + 2$ then

A $x < 1$ Ⓐ
B $x < 3$ Ⓑ
C $x > 1$ Ⓒ
D $x > 3$ Ⓓ

55 A car, travelling at an average speed of 60 km h^{-1}, leaves on a journey at 08:15 hours. If the journey is 330 km and the driver stops for a 15 minute lunch break and a further 15 minutes to fix a flat tyre, the time of arrival is

A   13:30 hours   Ⓐ
B   13:45 hours   Ⓑ
C   14:00 hours   Ⓒ
D   14:15 hours   Ⓓ

56 If $\tan^2 \theta = \frac{9}{16}$ then $\cos^2 \theta$ is exactly

A $\frac{5}{4}$ Ⓐ
B $\frac{4}{5}$ Ⓑ
C $\frac{3}{4}$ Ⓒ
D $\frac{16}{25}$ Ⓓ

57 $16 - 3 \times 4 \div 2 =$

A -8 Ⓐ
B   2   Ⓑ
C   10   Ⓒ
D   26   Ⓓ

58 If $f(x) = -3x^2$ then $f(-2) =$

A -12 Ⓐ
B -6 Ⓑ
C   6   Ⓒ
D   12   Ⓓ

59

The Venn diagram above illustrates two finite sets X and Y. Which of the following statements are true?

I $X \subset Y$
II $Y \subset X$
III $X \cap Y = Y$
IV $X \cup Y = X$

A   I and IV only   Ⓐ
B   II and III only   Ⓑ
C   II, III and IV only   Ⓒ
D   All of the above   Ⓓ

60 In a regular polygon, the size of each exterior angle is $22\frac{1}{2}°$. If each side of the polygon is 6 cm then its perimeter is

A   30 cm   Ⓐ
B   36 cm   Ⓑ
C   48 cm   Ⓒ
D   96 cm   Ⓓ

Answers

1	B	13	D	25	C	37	C	49	D
2	B	14	C	26	A	38	B	50	A
3	C	15	B	27	C	39	D	51	B
4	B	16	C	28	C	40	D	52	D
5	B	17	B	29	C	41	C	53	C
6	A	18	A	30	D	42	B	54	C
7	A	19	D	31	D	43	A	55	A
8	C	20	C	32	C	44	B	56	C
9	C	21	A	33	C	45	A	57	B
10	A	22	C	34	B	46	B	58	D
11	C	23	D	35	A	47	A	59	A
12	C	24	C	36	A	48	B	60	B

1	C	13	A	25	D	37	D	49	A
2	D	14	B	26	A	38	D	50	B
3	B	15	C	27	D	39	C	51	B
4	A	16	D	28	C	40	A	52	D
5	C	17	A	29	B	41	C	53	C
6	B	18	A	30	D	42	A	54	B
7	A	19	D	31	B	43	B	55	D
8	C	20	C	32	A	44	C	56	A
9	A	21	B	33	B	45	C	57	C
10	C	22	B	34	A	46	D	58	C
11	B	23	D	35	C	47	C	59	B
12	C	24	C	36	C	48	B	60	C

Test number 3

1 (D)	13 (D)	25 (D)	37 (C)	49 (D)
2 (C)	14 (C)	26 (D)	38 (C)	50 (D)
3 (A)	15 (D)	27 (D)	39 (B)	51 (C)
4 (B)	16 (A)	28 (C)	40 (A)	52 (A)
5 (D)	17 (A)	29 (B)	41 (C)	53 (B)
6 (C)	18 (B)	30 (B)	42 (A)	54 (C)
7 (A)	19 (D)	31 (A)	43 (B)	55 (B)
8 (B)	20 (B)	32 (C)	44 (C)	56 (C)
9 (D)	21 (C)	33 (B)	45 (A)	57 (D)
10 (B)	22 (C)	34 (A)	46 (B)	58 (B)
11 (B)	23 (C)	35 (B)	47 (D)	59 (A)
12 (C)	24 (A)	36 (D)	48 (B)	60 (B)

Test number 4

1 (D)	13 (D)	25 (C)	37 (B)	49 (B)
2 (C)	14 (C)	26 (D)	38 (D)	50 (C)
3 (D)	15 (D)	27 (B)	39 (A)	51 (A)
4 (D)	16 (B)	28 (D)	40 (D)	52 (D)
5 (B)	17 (C)	29 (A)	41 (C)	53 (B)
6 (B)	18 (A)	30 (A)	42 (C)	54 (D)
7 (C)	19 (D)	31 (D)	43 (A)	55 (B)
8 (C)	20 (B)	32 (C)	44 (B)	56 (C)
9 (D)	21 (A)	33 (C)	45 (C)	57 (C)
10 (A)	22 (B)	34 (C)	46 (C)	58 (D)
11 (A)	23 (D)	35 (C)	47 (D)	59 (B)
12 (B)	24 (B)	36 (B)	48 (B)	60 (C)

Test number 5

1	D	13	D	25	D	37	C	49	B
2	D	14	C	26	A	38	B	50	C
3	B	15	D	27	C	39	D	51	C
4	C	16	B	28	D	40	A	52	A
5	A	17	B	29	B	41	C	53	C
6	D	18	D	30	C	42	A	54	C
7	C	19	B	31	A	43	A	55	B
8	A	20	B	32	B	44	A	56	D
9	A	21	C	33	D	45	C	57	C
10	D	22	B	34	A	46	D	58	B
11	B	23	B	35	D	47	B	59	A
12	C	24	A	36	A	48	B	60	C

Test number 6

1	B	13	A	25	B	37	C	49	D
2	A	14	B	26	B	38	D	50	A
3	B	15	D	27	B	39	A	51	B
4	D	16	C	28	B	40	B	52	A
5	A	17	B	29	C	41	A	53	C
6	A	18	A	30	C	42	A	54	C
7	C	19	C	31	A	43	B	55	D
8	B	20	A	32	D	44	D	56	A
9	C	21	C	33	D	45	C	57	D
10	D	22	C	34	D	46	B	58	C
11	B	23	C	35	C	47	D	59	A
12	A	24	B	36	C	48	C	60	C

Test number ⑦

1	C	13	C	25	D	37	C	49	D
2	A	14	A	26	B	38	A	50	A
3	D	15	A	27	A	39	D	51	D
4	A	16	D	28	A	40	A	52	B
5	B	17	C	29	D	41	B	53	B
6	D	18	B	30	B	42	A	54	B
7	C	19	B	31	C	43	B	55	D
8	A	20	B	32	B	44	B	56	C
9	A	21	C	33	D	45	B	57	A
10	B	22	A	34	C	46	C	58	B
11	D	23	B	35	C	47	A	59	C
12	C	24	A	36	C	48	D	60	D

Test number ⑧

1	A	13	C	25	B	37	A	49	D
2	C	14	C	26	B	38	B	50	C
3	B	15	B	27	A	39	B	51	D
4	D	16	A	28	D	40	D	52	C
5	B	17	C	29	B	41	C	53	C
6	C	18	A	30	C	42	A	54	C
7	B	19	B	31	C	43	A	55	B
8	B	20	D	32	C	44	B	56	D
9	D	21	D	33	B	45	D	57	B
10	C	22	A	34	B	46	B	58	A
11	D	23	C	35	C	47	A	59	C
12	C	24	D	36	D	48	B	60	C

Test number 9

1	D	13	B	25	B	37	D	49	C
2	B	14	C	26	C	38	B	50	C
3	B	15	D	27	C	39	C	51	A
4	A	16	B	28	D	40	A	52	C
5	B	17	A	29	B	41	C	53	B
6	D	18	C	30	B	42	C	54	C
7	C	19	B	31	C	43	A	55	B
8	B	20	D	32	A	44	A	56	A
9	D	21	C	33	B	45	D	57	B
10	B	22	D	34	C	46	B	58	A
11	A	23	B	35	D	47	A	59	B
12	D	24	C	36	C	48	D	60	D

Test number 10

1	C	13	C	25	C	37	A	49	B
2	C	14	B	26	C	38	B	50	C
3	B	15	D	27	D	39	A	51	A
4	A	16	D	28	A	40	B	52	C
5	A	17	B	29	C	41	D	53	A
6	C	18	D	30	B	42	C	54	D
7	D	19	C	31	B	43	B	55	A
8	B	20	A	32	D	44	D	56	A
9	B	21	B	33	B	45	A	57	C
10	C	22	C	34	A	46	C	58	D
11	A	23	B	35	D	47	C	59	D
12	D	24	D	36	C	48	C	60	C

Test number 11

1	B	13	C	25	A	37	C	49	D
2	D	14	C	26	C	38	D	50	C
3	C	15	D	27	D	39	C	51	A
4	A	16	B	28	B	40	A	52	B
5	A	17	B	29	C	41	B	53	D
6	C	18	C	30	B	42	B	54	B
7	B	19	B	31	C	43	D	55	D
8	D	20	A	32	D	44	C	56	A
9	C	21	D	33	A	45	A	57	B
10	C	22	D	34	D	46	B	58	C
11	D	23	A	35	C	47	C	59	B
12	D	24	C	36	B	48	B	60	D

Test number 12

1	C	13	C	25	A	37	B	49	C
2	A	14	D	26	A	38	C	50	D
3	C	15	D	27	D	39	B	51	C
4	B	16	A	28	B	40	B	52	A
5	A	17	C	29	B	41	B	53	A
6	C	18	B	30	B	42	C	54	B
7	C	19	C	31	C	43	D	55	D
8	D	20	B	32	A	44	A	56	D
9	D	21	C	33	C	45	B	57	C
10	D	22	B	34	C	46	C	58	A
11	D	23	C	35	A	47	C	59	C
12	A	24	D	36	B	48	C	60	D